Fun Facts "For Better or Worse... But Mostly Bizarre"

The Hilarious, Heartbreaking, and Utterly Bewildering Ways Humans Have Formalized 'I do' and 'I don't Anymore' Across Civilizations.

Take it or Leave it.

NICCI BROCHARD
&
DR. BEN CHUBA

Fun Facts "For Better or Worse... But Mostly Bizarre"

The Hilarious, Heartbreaking, and Utterly Bewildering Ways Humans Have Formalized 'I do' and 'I don't Anymore' Across Civilizations.

Take it or Leave it.

CROSSBORDER

New York, London, Quebec

Contents

Introduction 1

Chapter 1: A Whale of a Courtship – Dowries, Curses, and Other Pre-Wedding Trials 3

Whale You Marry Me? – Fijian grooms must present a whale's tooth to win a bride's hand 3

Fat Chance of Wedlock – Mauritanian brides-to-be fatten up to please their future husbands 5

The Crying Game – In southwest China, Tujia brides weep for a month before the big day (tears of joy... allegedly) 7

Here Comes the Fake Bride – Russian families demand a proper dowry or send in a decoy bride until satisfied 9

Marry a Tree First, Honey – Cursed "Manglik" women in India wed a tree (then ax it) to break a bad-luck spell 11

Chapter 2: I Do (Don't Laugh) – Outlandish Wedding Ceremony Rituals 14

Poker-Faced "I Do" – In Congo the couple must not smile throughout the ceremony 14

Spit of Blessing – Maasai fathers in Kenya literally spit on their daughters at the altar for good luck 18

Filthy Fiancées – Scotland's "blackening" ritual ties up the bride and pelts her with rubbish to prep for marriage hardships 21

Fish Slaps and Sole Mates – Korean grooms get their feet whipped with fish by friends before the wedding night 24

Cupid's Missed Arrows – In China's Yugur culture, the groom fires three headless arrows at his bride, then breaks them to seal eternal love 27

Chapter 3: The Party's Just Getting Weird – Strange Post-Wedding Customs .. 32

Toilet Bowl Cocktail – In an old French tradition, wedding guests mix leftover food and drink in a toilet and demand the newlyweds chug it 32

Three-Day Lockdown – Borneo's Tidong newlyweds can't leave their room or use the bathroom for 72 hours after the wedding 34

The Kissing Commotion – In Sweden, if one newlywed leaves to use the restroom, the other gets mobbed with kisses by everyone left behind 36

Human Doormat – In the Marquesas Islands, relatives lie face-down so the bride and groom can literally walk on them as a post-ceremony sendoff 38

In-Law Chaperones – In Swahili culture, a village elder or the bride's mother may escort the couple to the bedroom to "advise" the bride on the wedding night 40

Chapter 4: Till Death and Beyond – Ghosts, Corpses, and Otherworldly Unions 44

Tomb-Mates – Ancient Chinese ghost weddings marry two deceased people (or even a living person to a dead one) so no soul travels lonely 44

The Ghost Groom – Among the Dinka and Nuer of South Sudan, a woman may marry a deceased man via his brother; children from the union are legally the dead man's heirs 46

Posthumous "I Do" – French law uniquely allows marrying a dead fiancé (with presidential approval), turning 'til death do us part on its head 48

Brotherly Backup – The ancient levirate custom required a widowed woman to marry her late husband's brother to keep it in the family (literally) 50

Holy Spouse – Nuns became "Brides of Christ," taking lifelong vows to marry God (complete with wedding rings and irreverent bridal metaphors in ceremony) 52

Chapter 5: Two's Company, Ten's a Crowd – Unconventional Marriage Arrangements 55

Solomon's 700 Club – Biblical King Solomon had 700 wives and 300 concubines, a harem so famous it's recorded in scripture 55

Brother-Husbands – In rural Tibet, fraternal polyandry lets one wife marry multiple brothers to keep family property intact 57

Free Love Commune – The 19th-century Oneida Community in New York practiced "complex marriage" where every man was married to every woman and vice versa 59

Nero's Nuptial Shenanigans – Roman Emperor Nero twice married men: taking one as his husband and later wedding a castrated boy as his wife in full imperial wedding pomp 61

World's Largest Family – Indian polygamist Ziona Chana left behind 39 wives and 94 children, running a household of 167 people under one roof 63

Chapter 6: Headaches and Headless Exes – Royal Breakups in History...........66

1. The Divorce Heard 'Round the Church – England's Henry VIII split from the Catholic Church (and Catherine of Aragon) when the Pope refused his divorce 67

2. Annulment by Axe – When Anne Boleyn didn't produce a male heir, Henry VIII solved the "divorce" by beheading her – talk about an extreme breakup .. 68

3. Queen Upgrades – Eleanor of Aquitaine annulled her marriage to Louis VII of France on convenient consanguinity grounds, then promptly married a younger, future king 70

4. No Divorce, No Problem – For centuries in Catholic Europe, clever nobles sought annulments (or exile to convents) to escape marriages, since divorce was off the table 73

5. Modern Crown Cracks – Even fairy-tale marriages fail: Britain's Charles and Diana's very public split in 1996 showed that not even royalty are guaranteed a happily ever after (no guillotine needed)... 76

Chapter 7: Un-tying the Knot, DIY-Style – Bizarre Divorce Customs of Common Folk 79

Packing His Bags – In old Cherokee and Hopi tradition, a wife could end the marriage by simply leaving her husband's belongings outside the home........... 80

Market Value – 18th-century English husbands literally sold their wives at the market with a rope around the wife's neck, auctioneer-style, as a makeshift divorce.. 82

"I Divorce Thee" x3 – The now-banned triple talaq allowed a Muslim man to instantly divorce his wife by saying "talaq" (I divorce you) three times – even via text 84

Ring Return Refund – Folklore in Merry Old England held that if a husband neglected his wife, she could dump him by handing back his ring, no court needed 87

When in Rome, Just Walk Away – In Ancient Rome, divorces were easy: spouses could dissolve the marriage by mutual consent (no lawyers, just ciao!), leading many Romans to have multiple exes by age 20 89

Chapter 8: Lawfully Wedded Weird – Outrageous Marriage Laws and Loopholes 92

Lawfully Wedded Weird – Outrageous Marriage Laws and Loopholes 92

Marrying the Dead – French necrogamy law (dating to WWI) lets you marry your deceased sweetheart under strict conditions 93

Proxy Knot-Tying – In Montana you can have a double proxy wedding: neither the bride nor groom shows up, and stand-ins get you legally hitched from afar 96

Mother-in-Law Insurance – Wichita, Kansas once required husbands to be nice to their mothers-in-law or it was legal grounds for divorce 100

Fowl Play – A 1770s law in Truro, Massachusetts demanded bachelors kill six blackbirds or three crows each before they were allowed to marry 103

Denture Disclosure – An old Vermont law made it illegal for a wife to get false teeth without her husband's written permission (toothless grin and bear it) .. 107

Chapter 9: Happily Never After – Modern Divorce Celebrations and Ceremonies 112

Divorce Cakes & Confetti – Celebrating Your Unwedding in Style 112

Ring Smash Bash – Japan's Formal Divorce Ceremony (Bring Your Own Mallet) 115

Weekend Divorce Getaway – Checking In Married, Checking Out Single (No Room Service Included) 119

Sologamy Self-Split – When You Divorce… Yourself (The Ultimate It's-Not-You-It's-Me) 123

Conscious Uncoupling – Splitting with Gwyneth Paltrow Spa Vibes (Goop-y Breakups) 127

Chapter 10: Stranger Than Fiction – The Bizarrest Odds and Ends of 'I Do' and 'I Don't' 133

Raining Cats, Frogs, and Goats – In parts of India, people have married frogs, dogs, even donkeys in elaborate ceremonies to ward off curses or summon rain 133

The Cursed Canine Groom – An Indian man once wed a dog to atone for killing two dogs years prior – a priest and 200 guests attended the ceremony to lift his "mutt" curse 136

Ladies' Privilege – According to Irish tradition (dating back to St. Patrick), every Leap Year on February 29 women can propose marriage to men – a custom that once even had legal force in Europe 139

Bachelor Tax – From Emperor Augustus's Rome to 20th-century governments, single men have been slapped with taxes for not marrying, as a not-so-subtle hint to get hitched 142

The Big "I Do" – In 1992, 20,825 couples said "I do" in unison at a Seoul stadium (with 9,800 more couples via satellite) in history's largest mass wedding – talk about married at first sight 146

Epilogue **151**

Introduction

Marriage: humanity's most enduring performance art, complete with costumes, vows that sound suspiciously like hostage negotiations, and audience members who secretly wonder if the open bar will compensate for sitting through another rendition of "The Wedding March." We've been doing this dance for millennia, and frankly, we've gotten spectacularly creative in our approaches to legally binding ourselves to another human being—sometimes multiple human beings, occasionally livestock, and in one documented case from medieval France, a deceased badger named Philippe.

Before you assume this collection celebrates the romantic institution that gave us diamond monopolies and the phrase "till death do us part" (originally "till debt do us part," but accountants make terrible poets), consider that humans have approached matrimony with the same innovative spirit they've applied to warfare, taxation, and reality television. The results range from heartwarming to horrifying, with frequent stops at completely unhinged.

Take the ancient Romans, who understood that marriage was essentially a business merger with better catering. Their prenuptials included clauses about which gods to worship, whose mother-in-law got visiting rights, and precisely how many olive trees constituted adequate dowry compensation. Meanwhile, medieval Europeans treated divorce like modern-day cryptocurrency trading—technically possible but requiring so much paperwork that most people simply waited for plague or childbirth to resolve their marital disputes naturally.

The Victorians, bless their repressed hearts, elevated wedding ceremonies to theatrical productions that would make Broadway producers weep with envy. They simultaneously created the white wedding dress (thanks, Queen Victoria, for making every bride since 1840 cosplay as you) and invented approximately forty-seven different ways to die of embarrassment during the reception.

But humans weren't content to limit their matrimonial creativity to mere ceremony. We've developed divorce laws that read like satirical fiction, custody arrangements that require advanced degrees in diplomacy, and prenuptial agreements that make corporate mergers look like playground handshake deals.

This compendium documents humanity's most inspired moments of matrimonial madness, from cultures that required grooms to prove their worthiness by surviving snake bites to societies where divorce required formal presentations to councils of elders, complete with visual aids and character witnesses.

Prepare yourself for a journey through love's greatest hits and most spectacular failures, where romance meets bureaucracy, and "happily ever after" comes with terms and conditions that nobody bothered to read.

Ben and I (Nicci) are excited about this book. We hope you laugh and learn. Thank you in advance for choosing our book.

Chapter 1

A Whale of a Courtship – Dowries, Curses, and Other Pre-Wedding Trials

Whale You Marry Me? – Fijian grooms must present a whale's tooth to win a bride's hand

Weddings are supposed to celebrate love. But in some places, before you get to the "happily ever after," you've got to jump through hoops that make juggling in-laws and seating charts look like child's play. Case in point: In Fiji, if a guy wants to pop the question for real, he might need to pop open a whale's mouth first. Yes, you read that right.

Forget the diamond ring – Fijian tradition says a groom must present his future father-in-law with a whale's tooth. It's called a *tabua*, and it's basically a hall pass to marry the daughter. Now, I know what you're thinking: *"Is a whale's tooth easier to get than, say, a blessing on Twitter from Chrissy Teigen?"* Hard to say. But it certainly raises the bar for *"meeting the parents"* nerves.

Imagine the scene: our nervous groom (let's call him Sireli) shows up at his girlfriend's village, carrying the customary gifts, and hidden in a woven bag he's got… a giant curved whale tooth. It looks like something from Moby Dick's dentist or an artifact Indiana Jones would risk his fedora for. Sireli kneels before the bride's father and offers this colossal incisor as if to say, *"I promise I'm serious about your daughter – look, I wrestled a sea monster for her!"* It's dramatic, it's touching, and it probably makes every Western dude with a Neil Lane ring feel a tad underdressed. After all, how many of them literally bring teeth to the negotiating table?

For the record, no whales are harmed in modern times for this token – these teeth are treasured heirlooms, passed down like Grandma's engagement ring (if Grandma were an orca). Still, the symbolism is wild. A whale's tooth is a sign of honor and value, basically saying *"your daughter is so precious, I scoured the ocean for something equally rare."* Extreme, yes – but oddly sweet, if you think about it. It sure beats clicking "Buy Now" on Amazon for a nice kitchen appliance, right?

This tradition makes for some entertaining modern-day what-ifs. Picture a would-be groom from New York falling for a Fijian girl. One minute he's picking out a ring, the next he's scouring eBay for whale teeth and cold-calling marine biologists. (You thought finding the right ring was tough – try sourcing oceanic ivory on a deadline.) If rom-coms were realistic, we'd have at least one montage of a guy sneaking through a natural history museum after hours, Mission Impossible-style, to "borrow" a whale molar for love.

Talk about making a big gesture – literally. We've all heard the phrase "go big or go home." In Fiji, you go big *to* go home with your bride. A whale is one of the biggest creatures on Earth, so offering a part of one says, *"My love for you is gigantic, and I have the dental evidence to prove it."* Every relationship has hurdles; in Fiji, one of those hurdles just happens to weigh several tons and swim in the Pacific.

Marriage lesson? Commitment sometimes means doing the outrageous. If you can secure a whale's tooth to win your love, you're probably going to survive the trials of assembling Ikea furniture or deciding whose relatives to visit for Christmas. Consider it early training. It sets the tone: "Honey, I literally faced a whale for you – taking out the trash on Tuesdays is nothing." And once Dad is happy with his shiny whale tooth, the hardest part is over. The rest of the wedding is smooth sailing… unless someone forgets the kava bowl, but that's another story.

So next time you roll your eyes at over-the-top engagement demands (looking at you, folks proposing via helicopter over the Grand Canyon), spare a thought for the Fijian groom with his whale tooth dowry. He may not have gone ring shopping at Tiffany's, but he's got a heck of a story – and an offbeat keepsake for the mantle. Hey, at least a whale's tooth never needs resizing!

Fat Chance of Wedlock – Mauritanian brides-to-be fatten up to please their future husbands

If you thought squeezing into a wedding dress after months of diet shakes was hard, Mauritania has a plot twist for you. In this West African nation, some brides-to-be do the exact opposite of the keto bridal bootcamp. That's right – they're fattening up like it's an Olympic event and the gold medal is a happily ever after. In a world of Instagram filters and "shedding for the wedding" juice cleanses, these ladies are out here chugging full-fat camel's milk and singing, "I like big butts and I cannot lie," without a hint of irony.

It's rooted in the idea that a fuller figure signals wealth, beauty, and prosperity. Skinny? Oh no. In traditional Mauritanian culture, a thin bride might even be a slight on the groom's reputation – how can he provide if his bride isn't, well, visibly well-fed?

So families, especially in rural areas, historically sent their young daughters to fattening farms (yes, that's a thing). Under the watchful eye of an auntie-turned-drill-sergeant, these girls consume gargantuan quantities of food. We're talking 10,000 calories a day or more – pounded millet, rich meats, endless bowls of sweet camel milk. Imagine a buffet that never closes, and you're not allowed to leave until you've had fourths.

The pressure to plump up can be intense. It's basically Bridezilla meets Supersize Me. Aunties will threaten, cajole, even employ the occasional stick-whack on a stubborn toe to ensure that bowl of buttery couscous is licked clean. It's tough love to the extreme – the kind that makes your own grandma's insistence on second helpings look like amateur hour. ("You're looking too thin, eat!" is a universal refrain, but Mauritanian grannies turn it up to eleven.)

On the plus side (pun intended), a Mauritanian bride isn't stressing about squeezing into a size 2 gown – she's proudly embracing every curve, and her gown will be tailored to *her.* You can bet the wedding feast is going to be epic, because this bride has trained like a competitive eater for the big day.

And consider the marital prep happening here: patience, resilience, and the ability to find joy (or at least tolerance) in whatever life, or Auntie Fatima, piles on your plate. In a world obsessed with shedding pounds, there's something almost refreshing about this extreme opposite approach. It's a reminder that beauty truly is relative

– one culture's "lose a pound" is another's "gain ten!" Maybe the happiest couples are the ones who can say, "I loved you at any size and I have the empty ice cream tubs to prove it."

The Crying Game – In southwest China, Tujia brides weep for a month before the big day (tears of joy… allegedly)

Everyone expects a few tears on the wedding day – the groom choking up, Mom dabbing her eyes, even Dad getting misty during the father-daughter dance. But one part of China says: why limit the waterworks to a single day? The Tujia people of southwest China have a pre-wedding tradition that takes "crying your eyes out" to a whole new level. Tujia brides don't just cry at the ceremony – they cry *before* the ceremony, every day for a month leading up to it. Call it a marathon of melodrama, an Olympiad of weeping.

Picture a bride-to-be, we'll call her Lin, marking her calendar: 30 days to go, time to start the nightly cry-fest. About one hour each evening, like clockwork, she sits down and sobs. For the first week, she cries solo, channeling all the bittersweet feelings of leaving home. After that, her mother joins in – now it's a duet of boo-hoos. A few days later, Grandma shuffles in, presumably thinking "I've waited decades to have a good cry with you." Before long, every aunt, sister, and female cousin in the vicinity has joined the sob squad. By the end of the month, it's a full-blown chorus of tears – a daily bonding ritual that leaves the whole house looking like the audience at the end of *Titanic*.

Believe it or not, these are tears of joy (or so the tradition says). The crying is meant to express happiness, gratitude, and all the warm fuzzies about the upcoming union – translated in Tujia terms as a river of tears. In fact, if done properly, the weeping eventually takes on a musical cadence. Different family members cry in different tones, supposedly creating a layered melody of misery. (Who needs karaoke when you have a month-long sob fest?)

To outsiders, this sounds like an absolute spectacle. Walk in around week three and you'd think tragedy struck. *"Did the wedding get called off? Did someone die?"* Nope – just the family getting their happy cries on. It's baffling and oddly heartwarming at the same time.

On one hand, you've got a month of puffy eyes and probably a permanent tissue box fixture on the coffee table. On the other, it's kind of sweet that the family is so tight-knit they'll literally cry together in anticipation of a joyful event.

Silver lining: by the time the wedding rolls around, the bride has no tears left to cry. She's already vented every possible emotion. (Compared to orchestrating nightly sob sessions, dealing with a caterer snafu or seating chart debacle is a piece of cake.) Plus, the family that cries together laughs together – eventually. There's a unique closeness forged in those shared weepy hours, like an intense pre-wedding therapy that costs nothing but tissues.

And perhaps there's a lesson here: embrace the emotions, don't bottle them up. Marriage is a big life change; the Tujia just take an all-in approach to confronting that fact. By flooding the house with tears, they cleanse away sadness and fear, leaving a clean slate for the bride's new chapter. Sure, it's dramatic (on a soap-opera scale), but it certainly makes for a memorable kickoff to married life.

For any over-stressed bride (or groom), the takeaway might be to let yourself have a good cry when you need it. Maybe don't schedule 30 days of it – your boss might not approve – but a pre-wedding cry-sesh or two could be just the stress relief you need. At the very least, it'll give you a great story: "Oh yeah, I was so ready for marriage, my whole family and I cried for weeks beforehand – *on purpose.*"

Here Comes the Fake Bride – Russian families demand a proper dowry or send in a decoy bride until satisfied

Just when you thought you'd heard every crazy in-law story, let's chat about Russian weddings. Specifically, a tradition that sounds like a mashup of *The Godfather* and *Mrs. Doubtfire.* Back in the day (and occasionally still today, for laughs), a Russian bride's family had a creative way to negotiate the dowry or "bride price": if they found the offer a bit underwhelming, they wouldn't haggle – they'd hoodwink. The eager groom shows up ready to claim his beloved, only to be met with a fake bride. That's right – the family presents a decoy in a wedding dress, and not a very convincing one at that.

Imagine our poor groom, Ivan, standing at the door with flowers and champagne, all excited to see his beautiful bride. Suddenly, out comes "Natalia." But Natalia looks… off. Is that a mustache under the veil? Indeed it is – it's the bride's burly cousin Boris in a dress, grinning like Cinderella's hairy godmother. The family bursts into laughter and declares, "*Nyet, not enough! Try again, and bring a better gift this time.*" In other words: your dowry didn't impress, so we're keeping the real bride in the back room until you pony up a bit more cash or goodies.

This prank is part of the Russian *vykup nevesty*, or "bride ransom." Nowadays it's usually done playfully to give everyone a good chuckle and the groom a mild heart attack. Think of it as an interactive improv game at the groom's expense. The bridesmaids or relatives might set up other silly challenges too: trivia about the bride ("Prove you know her middle name or pay 100 rubles!"), goofy dares, or the classic test where they cover a poster with lipstick kisses and the poor guy must guess which kiss is his fiancée's. (Pro tip: compliment every guesser – you score points with all the ladies.)

But the pièce de résistance is always the fake bride gag. It's comedy gold for the guests and a moment of pure mortification for the groom. After enough games and *ahem* financial incentives, the family decides that Ivan has proved his devotion (and fattened the wedding fund enough). At last, they reveal the real bride – who's likely been peeking from behind a door, trying not to snort with laughter while her man is jumping through hoops.

If a couple can get through this, they can get through pretty much anything. I mean, what's a forgotten anniversary compared to literally negotiating for your spouse with chocolates and rubles while Uncle Boris bats his falsies at you? In a weird way, this quirky ordeal is the family's way of saying *"Welcome, we love you – now prove you love us (and her) back."* It's hazing, but make it Slavic.

And hidden in the humor is a solid piece of advice: be ready to improvise and roll with the punches. Marriage will throw surprises at you – maybe not a cross-dressing cousin, but curveballs nonetheless. A sense of humor and a willingness to play along go a long way in any partnership (especially when in-laws are involved). Also, note to self:

never underestimate what a family will do to make a point. Drama isn't reserved for the bride – sometimes it's the whole squad.

So if you ever find yourself about to tie the knot Russian-style, come prepared. Perhaps tuck an extra envelope of cash in your jacket, plaster a grin on your face, and double-check under that veil for rogue mustaches. Do that, and you'll pass their test with flying colors.

Marry a Tree First, Honey – Cursed "Manglik" women in India wed a tree (then ax it) to break a bad-luck spell

Our final stop on this wild wedding ride dives into the realm of astrology, superstition, and... gardening. In India, love isn't only in the air – it's in the stars, written into horoscopes. And if those stars aren't aligned just right, you might have to tie the knot with a tree before you can marry your actual fiancé. It sounds like a prank, but it's a real custom practiced as a remedy for what some call a cosmic curse. Enter the concept of the Manglik bride.

Being "Manglik" means you were born under a certain astrological condition (blame an ill-positioned Mars) that supposedly dooms your spouse to an early grave. Yeah, not exactly a selling point on your Tinder profile – "Swipe right at your own risk; I might hex you." To avoid turning hubby into an early ghost, the idea is: marry a tree first.

Yes, a literal tree – often a peepal or banana tree will do. The belief is that this first, sacrificial marriage absorbs the curse. The tree gets whacked by the bad juju, allowing the once-cursed woman to marry her human love without any lingering death omens.

11

So, in practice, a full wedding ceremony is performed with the tree as the stand-in groom. Picture a lovely outdoor wedding… except the groom has roots and bark. Vows are (symbolically) exchanged, maybe a garland is draped around the trunk, and at least the groom's family doesn't cause drama (unless Greenpeace counts). Then, once the "I dos" are done, it's time for the finale: the tree "husband" is cut down. Timber! The curse is declared broken, and everyone breathes a sigh of relief (except maybe the tree, may it rest in pieces).

This ritual, called *kumbh vivah*, isn't hugely common but is well-known enough that even celebrities have been linked to it. Bollywood superstar Aishwarya Rai was rumored to have married a tree before her actual wedding, just to be safe. She later chuckled at the gossip, but the fact people bought the story shows how ingrained this belief can be (and how much folks love a bizarre celebrity headline).

On one hand, it's quite the romantic gesture: *"I love you so much I'll commit arboreal bigamy to protect you from my evil stars."* That's some next-level dedication. On the other hand, it's a tad dramatic – a bit like doing an exorcism on your love life. But who are we to judge? When it comes to securing a happily-ever-after, people have done stranger things (okay, maybe marrying a tree is near the top of the strange list).

Does science back this up? Nah. Do a lot of modern Indians roll their eyes at this? Absolutely. Yet, when weddings and deep-rooted beliefs collide, many figure, hey, *why risk it?* You only (hopefully) marry once – might as well appease every deity, planet, and old wives' tale. Call it spiritual insurance. And if nothing else, it makes for an excellent icebreaker at parties. ("Fun fact: I'm technically a widow. No, no, he was a tree.")

If there's a takeaway from this arboreal adventure, it's that every couple does what makes them feel secure. Marriage has plenty of real challenges – finances, in-laws, thermostat battles – so if a quirky ritual eases your mind, more power to you. Chop that tree, dunk that curse, and then maybe plant a new sapling as an apology to Mother Nature.

From whales to waistlines, tears to trickery, and even tying the knot with timber, love truly makes people do bizarre and wonderful things. Sure, these customs are wild and make for great cocktail-party anecdotes, but under the surface they share a common heartbeat: everyone just wants a happily-ever-after, whatever it takes. As we laugh at these stories, we might nod in understanding – we all go a little overboard making our big day special (though maybe not *whale tooth and sacrificial tree* overboard). In the end, these pre-wedding trials are simply extreme ways of saying *"I'd do anything for love."* And if nothing else, they guarantee one heck of a wedding tale. Years down the road, when the grandkids ask how you tied the knot, you might just lean back and begin with, "Well, there was this whale's tooth and a tree, and then Uncle Boris showed up in a dress..." – topping any love story they've ever heard.

Chapter 2

I Do (Don't Laugh) – Outlandish Wedding Ceremony Rituals

Weddings are supposed to be romantic, elegant, and joyous occasions – but who says they can't also be bizarre, messy, or downright laugh-out-loud weird? In this chapter, we're taking a trip down the aisle less traveled, to explore some of the most outlandish wedding ceremony rituals from around the world. Buckle up (or, um, veil up?), because by the end you might just be grateful your biggest wedding worry was a drunk uncle on the dance floor. Our journey features poker-faced newlyweds, spitting fathers, garbage-covered brides, fish-whipped grooms, and an archer groom channeling Cupid (with questionable aim). It's a wild ride, told in a breezy, irreverent tone – think travelogue meets stand-up comedy, with a dash of marriage counseling. So grab a slice of wedding cake to snack on and prepare to say "I do" to some seriously bizarre traditions.

Poker-Faced "I Do" – In Congo the couple must not smile throughout the ceremony

Let's start our adventure in the heart of Africa, where the first rule of *Fight Club*—oops, I mean Congolese Wedding Club—is: you do not smile at Congolese Wedding Club. Yes, in the Democratic Republic of Congo, the bride and groom are required to get married looking like they're attending a particularly dull board meeting rather than the happiest day of their lives. No grins, no giggles, not even a tiny smirk. The couple must remain stone-faced from the moment they say "I do" until the ceremony is over (some even say until the entire wedding day is done and dusted). Imagine trying to do that while your giddy aunties are ululating with joy, a toddler ring bearer is picking his nose, and your college buddy in the front row is crossing his eyes trying to get you to crack. Nope – the happy couple has to channel their inner Buckingham Palace guard and keep that poker face intact.

Why such a serious vibe? Because marriage in Congo is serious business, and they mean it. The tradition holds that if you're grinning like a fool on your wedding day, you're clearly not taking this lifelong commitment seriously enough. (Sorry, Joker – this is one party you wouldn't fit in at.) In Western weddings, photographers shout "Say cheese!" to get everyone smiling, but a Congolese wedding photographer might as well say "Say Cameroon" – anything *but* cheese. The result? Wedding photos that look like yearbook pictures from a very strict school. The bride could be decked out in the most gorgeous gown, the groom in a dapper suit, but both of them will be serving Blue Steel looks all day long. Guests might be dancing, singing, maybe someone's doing the Macarena, but the newlyweds will be deadpan, as if they're practicing for an Olympic no-smiling contest.

It's equal parts impressive and intimidating. Picture this: the groom's mischievous little brother accidentally drops the wedding rings or the bride's BFF makes a ridiculous inside joke during her reading – and nobody laughs. Not a peep from the couple. Kim Kardashian's famously emotionless face has nothing on a Congolese bride determined to follow tradition. Even Kanye (who once said he tries not to smile in photos because it's not cool) would find this tradition extreme. You can almost hear the internal monologue of the bride: *"Must. Not. Laugh. Grandma's dancing the tango with my college roommate… keep it together!"* The self-control is admirable. I mean, most of us can't get through a work Zoom meeting without at least a polite smile, and here are two people experiencing one of the most joyous milestones of their lives with the solemnity of a Supreme Court swearing-in.

But let's give this tradition its due – hidden beneath the humor of watching a no-smile wedding is a nugget of wisdom about marriage. It underscores that marriage is a serious commitment, not just an excuse for a party and goofy photos. In an age where some weddings are basically Instagram photo-ops (with brides saying "Make sure you get my good side" and grooms choreographing viral dance moves down the aisle), there's something refreshing, if a bit hardcore, about a custom that says: *Hey, focus. This is important.* It's as if the Congolese custom is reminding couples that the gravity of the moment outweighs the frills and giggles. Sure, it might be a buzzkill for the Best Man's stand-up routine during the vows, but it certainly trains the couple in united stoicism. After all, life will throw plenty of curveballs at you post-wedding – if you can get through your entire wedding day while Uncle Didier is doing the chicken dance without cracking a grin, you can probably handle jointly doing your taxes or not laughing when your partner-to-be trips over the doorstep carrying you.

Of course, one imagines that once the ceremony is over and they're officially hitched, the couple must breathe a huge sigh of relief and then burst into smiles (or at least go in a back room and massage their face muscles because wow, those cheeks must be sore from suppression). Perhaps later at the reception, when the rule relaxes, the new husband and wife finally let loose – maybe they even overcompensate with extra beaming and laughing, catching up for all those stifled chuckles. It's like the wedding version of that challenge where you try not to laugh at a ridiculous video; except the "video" is real life, and it's your wedding.

In a way, a Congolese no-smile ceremony could be the ultimate relationship test. Can we enjoy a deeply meaningful moment together without the need for performative grinning? Can we communicate joy through our eyes alone, or through meaningful glances, while keeping a straight face? If the answer is yes, then that couple might just have the patience and understanding to navigate married life. At the very least, their grandkids will one day ask, "Grandma, why do you look so mad in your wedding pictures? Didn't you love Grandpa?" And she'll have a great story to tell – about how not laughing at Grandpa's terrible jokes on day one was actually a *cultural requirement*, not a reflection of her feelings.

So next time you attend a wedding and the bride and groom are grinning ear to ear, spare a thought for the couples in Congo pulling off the ultimate straight-faced stunt. It's a testament to self-control, cultural values, and maybe a hint of "we dare you to make us laugh" bravado. In the grand theater of weddings, where most couples can't stop smiling, these two deserve an Oscar for Best Serious Performance in a Romantic Ceremony. And if you ask me, the minute it's over, they've earned the right to laugh for a lifetime – together.

Spit of Blessing – Maasai fathers in Kenya literally spit on their daughters at the altar for good luck

Just when you thought it was safe to attend a wedding without a raincoat, let's hop over to Kenya and Tanzania, where the Maasai people have a tradition that might make even the most stoic bride say, "You're gonna do *what* now, Dad?!" In Maasai culture, when a daughter is getting married, her father doesn't shed a tear of joy – nope, he spits on her. Yes, you read that correctly: dear old dad gathers some saliva and lets it fly right onto his little girl's head or even her dress as she stands at the altar. It's his special way of saying, "Congrats, honey, and best of luck in your marriage!" Cue the bride's inner monologue: *"Love you too, Dad... I guess?"*

Now, for most of us, being spit on is about as appealing as stepping in a fresh cow pie on your way to the reception. It triggers an immediate eww reflex. But among the Maasai, this spitting ritual is anything but insult – it's considered a heartfelt blessing. In their cultural context, spitting can mean respect and good fortune. Maasai elders spit on newborn babies to bless them, and Maasai men even spit in their palms before a handshake as a sign of goodwill. So for a father to spit on his daughter as she leaves to start a new life is his way of leaving her with a protective coat of parental blessing (a very wet, drippy coat, but a blessing nonetheless). Think of it as the Maasai equivalent of a father's kiss on the forehead – except, well, a bit messier.

Let's set the scene: The bride is radiant in her traditional clothes and jewelry, maybe a beaded necklace gleaming in the sun. She's probably a bundle of nerves and excitement. Her father stands before her, perhaps with a bittersweet smile (unlike our Congo couple, smiling is allowed here!). He wants to wish her prosperity, many children, a happy life. So naturally, he hocks up a nice glob of spit and patooey! – lands it right on her head. Depending on dad's aim, it might dribble down her face or onto that gorgeous wedding necklace. And here's the kicker – the bride is supposed to not wipe it off. She walks off with glistening spit on her as a charm of good luck. It's like wearing your dad's love proudly... if your dad's love were a bodily fluid.

For any Western bride, this scenario is the stuff of nightmares – imagine spending hours on your hair and makeup, only for your father to essentially do a not-so-dry "water blessing" on you in front of all your guests. But a Maasai bride, raised with this tradition, likely takes it in stride. Perhaps she's even comforted by it: as gross as it might sound, it's her father's way of showing he cares deeply. In a sense, he's symbolically saying, "I hope the blessings stick to you like this spit." It's quite poetic if you squint past the ick factor.

From a humorous standpoint, this ritual is ripe for comedic analogies. For instance, we could say that Maasai weddings come with a built-in *"splash zone"* – guests in the front row, watch out, you might get hit with friendly fire! The father's got one shot at this, and hopefully he's got good aim and enough hydration. (Note to Maasai dads: maybe go easy on the pre-wedding salt tea, you don't want a Sahara-dry mouth when it's go-time.) It's also a twist on the classic phrase "I spit on your grave," turning it into "I spit on your wedding gown – with love." Who knew saliva could carry such sentimental weight?

Contemporary cultural reference check: Can you imagine this catching on in Hollywood? Picture a celebrity dad like, say, Billy Ray Cyrus at Miley's wedding, leaning in not for a hug but for a hearty spit on her head. The tabloids would implode. Or think of a political satire scenario: some diplomat greeting another with a spit handshake at the UN – probably not coming soon to international customs, but hey, it works for the Maasai! It definitely puts our mundane father-of-the-bride traditions into perspective. (Walking down the aisle and lifting the veil seem downright tame now, don't they?)

Underneath the layer of humor (and spittle), there's an oddly touching lesson here about marriage and family. The spit is a symbol that as the bride steps into her new life, she carries her father's blessing, however unorthodox its delivery. It's a reminder that love isn't always neat and tidy. In fact, sometimes love (and marriage) is messy – figuratively and literally. One day you're swapping rings and cutting cake; the next you're arguing over whose turn it is to do dishes or clean the baby's spit-up. The Maasai just get a head start on the mess, with a parental seal of approval that says, "May you have good fortune, and here's a little something to remember me by – DNA included."

So, if you find yourself at a Maasai wedding, don't be alarmed when you see the father of the bride clearing his throat meaningfully. Resist the urge to offer him a tissue – he's not getting choked up with tears, he's gathering ammo for a blessing. And when that spit flies, know that you are witnessing a tender, if unconventional, moment of parental love. It may not be Pinterest-worthy, but it's genuine. In the grand tapestry of global weddings, this tradition teaches us that a father's blessing can come in many forms. Sometimes it's a whispered prayer, sometimes a teary hug… and sometimes it's a well-aimed glob of spit landing smack on your fancy bridal beadwork. Cheers to that, and pass the hand sanitizer (just kidding)!

Filthy Fiancées – Scotland's "blackening" ritual ties up the bride and pelts her with rubbish to prep for marriage hardships

If you thought a little spit was gnarly, allow me to introduce you to a tradition from bonnie Scotland that takes "trash talk" to a whole new level. It's called "blackening the bride", and no, it's not a bizarre tanning ritual or a goth wedding theme. This is a pre-wedding tradition where the bride (and sometimes the groom, but let's be real, the bride usually gets the worst of it) is literally turned into a human garbage canvas by her loving friends and family. Yes, you read that correctly: the guest list basically becomes a mob of gleeful trash-throwers. Talk about filthy fiancées!

Here's how it typically goes down (brace yourself – it's a messy story): The bride is ambushed by her friends and relatives a few days before the wedding. They seize her, perhaps tie her up or secure her to a handy object like a tree or a pole (nothing says "we love you" like mild kidnapping), and then they proceed to pelt her with the grossest assortment of gunk they can concoct. We're talking rotten eggs, spoiled milk, curdled yogurt, fish guts, flour, mud, treacle (that's sticky syrup), feathers, and whatever else is festering in the back of the fridge. If it's slimy, grimy, or smelly, it's going on the bride. By the end of this onslaught, our poor bride looks less like a princess and more like a swamp creature emerging from a dumpster dimension. She is blackened – not just metaphorically, but often literally covered head to toe in black, brown, and neon yellow (egg yolk) splotches of yuck.

One imagines the commentary from bystanders: "Ach, doesn't she look lovely? That shade of garbage really brings out the color of her eyes!" It's the ultimate anti-bridezilla treatment – no one, not even the most diva bride, can stay prissy when she's got week-old fish scales in her hair. And that's kind of the point. This Scottish tradition is meant to humble the bride (and groom, if he's equally unlucky) and prepare them for the trials of married life. The logic is, if you can handle being publicly humiliated and disgustingly dirty while your nearest and dearest laugh their heads off, you can handle whatever challenges marriage throws your way. Think of it as a hardcore pre-marital boot camp, but instead of sit-ups and trust falls, it's "endure the rotten porridge flung at your face."

Of course, from a comedic angle, the whole scenario is pure slapstick gold (for everyone except the bride in the moment). It's like an over-the-top Nickelodeon slime episode meets *Braveheart*. Freedom! – for people to throw junk at you. The bride's expression (somewhere beneath the banana peel hanging off her ear) might range from hysterical laughter to "I am plotting revenge on every single one of you." And revenge is sometimes served: I've heard tales of brides who, after a thorough hosing off, come back with a super-soaker or a bucket of something vile to return the favor to her pals. Because true friendship, like marriage, is a two-way street of *shared chaos.*

Let's talk public spectacle: After the blackening ritual, it's not uncommon to parade the muck-covered bride around town. Yes, they take her on a little tour so everyone can witness her stylish new look. Perhaps they'll stop by the local pub, where regulars raise a pint to the sight of a bride dripping molasses and feathered like a broken pillow. It's practically a community event – nothing brings folks together like laughing at someone wearing garbage couture. If this sounds like a medieval punishment, you're not far off; being tarred and feathered comes to mind, except this is done out of affection (supposedly). Leave it to the Scots to spin an act of public humiliation into a pre-wedding party. It's simultaneously horrifying and heartwarming – *heartyfying*, if you will.

Imagine if we tried to pull this stunt in a celebrity wedding scenario. Let's say at Priyanka Chopra's wedding, her bridesmaids tie her up and dump last week's curry on her, followed by feathers from Nick Jonas's favorite pillow. Or picture an A-list Hollywood bride like Scarlett Johansson getting doused in spoiled milk and fish heads by her Avengers co-stars as a send-off to matrimony. The internet would break in half. But in certain Scottish villages, this is just Thursday night. As irreverent as it sounds, the tradition has deep roots and still survives (mostly in rural areas, and likely after a hearty amount of whisky for courage all around).

Now, the marriage lesson here – aside from "maybe keep a change of clothes handy" – is actually kind of sweet in its own twisted way. Marriage, as anyone who's been in one can attest, isn't all sunshine and synchronized dances. There will be hard times, messy times, moments you feel you're figuratively stuck to a tree and life is throwing rotten eggs at you. The Scottish blackening ritual basically says to the couple: If you can laugh off this literal mess, you can handle the figurative mess later. It builds resilience (not to mention a strong stomach). And importantly, it shows the couple that they have a community of loved ones who are total goofballs but will stand by them through thick and thin (and through sludge and stench). After all, those same friends who just showered you in garbage are going to be the ones dancing at your wedding, toasting to your future, and probably telling this story in their reception speech to thoroughly embarrass you one more time.

In a modern context, I've seen some couples do a light version of this – maybe a "trash the dress" photoshoot where the bride wades into the ocean or splashes paint on her gown. Cute, artsy, but kiddie pool stuff compared to the blackening. The Scots chuckle at such tame antics: "Call that a mess? Back in my day, we used *real* cow manure!" All in good fun, of course.

So here's to the brave brides (and grooms) of Scotland who take "getting trashed before the wedding" literally. They prove that sometimes the best way to enter a marriage is not in pristine perfection, but in outrageous, muddy, smelly solidarity with your partner. Because if you can face each other after seeing (and smelling) your absolute worst, 'til death do you part will be a piece of (heavily soiled) cake.

Fish Slaps and Sole Mates – Korean grooms get their feet whipped with fish by friends before the wedding night

As our global tour of wacky weddings continues, you might be thinking, "Surely the groom isn't spared from bizarre pre-wedding hijinks, right?" Fear not, dear reader – we now arrive in South Korea, where the groom's buddies have cooked up a ritual that ensures he quite literally gets cold feet – or perhaps "stinging feet" is more accurate. It's time to meet the custom of beating the groom's feet, often with a fish, because nothing says "Congrats on your marriage" like a good old-fashioned sole-whipping by your best friends.

Here's how this fin-tastic ritual plays out: After the wedding ceremony, before the groom can whisk away his bride for the wedding night, his groomsmen grab him for a little surprise. They remove his shoes and socks, tie his ankles together, and sometimes even hoist him up or pin him down so he can't squirm away (the groom at this point is probably thinking, "With friends like these, who needs enemies?"). Then they take turns whacking the soles of his feet with something – often a dried fish (a popular choice is a dried yellow corvina, if you want the full menu) or sometimes a stick or cane. Thwack, thwack! The groom yelps or laughs – likely a mix of both, as it's usually painful but more *awkward* and ticklish than truly injurious.

Now you may ask, why a fish?! Did someone look at a floppy dead fish and think, "Ah yes, the perfect tool to smack my pal's feet"? One explanation is that the fish adds an element of ridiculousness – it's meant to be more amusing than torturous. (Also, imagine the smell. The groom's feet are gonna have a lovely eau de seafood going into the honeymoon. Hopefully his new wife really, *really* likes sushi.) Another theory: this is a test of the groom's character and endurance. In some cases, as they beat his feet, the friends will quiz him, shouting trivia questions or asking, "What's your bride's birthday?" or "What's the price of the dowry, buddy?" The idea is to make sure he can keep his wits about him under pressure – a skill you definitely need when your spouse asks something like "Notice anything different about me?" and you better answer correctly even if you're distracted.

From a comedic standpoint, the whole scene is absurd in the best way. The groom, likely a bit tipsy from the reception, is now howling and flailing while his pals laugh maniacally and a dead fish goes *smack! smack!* on his soles. It's like a hazing ritual meets a Monty Python skit. (In fact, Monty Python once had a famous "fish-slapping dance" – the Koreans have turned it into a marital exam.) You half expect a British narrator to chime in: "And now for something completely different – a groom getting tenderized like tomorrow's sashimi."

Pop culture reference opportunity: If Quentin Tarantino (notorious for his cinematic foot obsessions) directed a romance, he might appreciate this scene – although he'd probably insist on a live octopus or something for extra shock value. Or picture a K-pop music video, all those suave boyband members, ending with them tying up the lead singer groom and merrily beating his feet with a mackerel in rhythm to the beat. It hasn't happened yet, but hey, BTS, call me – I've got concepts.

Now, does this ritual have a deeper meaning or is it just an excuse for the groomsmen to punk their friend? Officially, some say it's to make sure the groom won't get cold feet (because his feet hurt too much to run, get it?). Others claim it's to prepare him for the realities of marriage – a sort of "you think this hurts? Wait till you have to assemble IKEA furniture with your spouse at 2 AM." It's also framed as a way to wish fertility and strength; perhaps the stinging feet are supposed to invigorate the groom for, ahem, the wedding night activities. (Nothing like throbbing foot pain to really set the mood, fellas. Nice job.)

Marriage insight time: In a twisted way, this ritual says, *"buddy, marriage might pinch a bit, but you'll survive with a smile (and maybe a limp)."* It's also about trust and friendship. The groom allows his closest friends to put him in a vulnerable (and ridiculous) position, possibly because those same friends will be the support system he leans (or hops) on in married life. They're basically saying, "We've got your back – today we're whacking your feet, but tomorrow we'll help you move furniture into your new home. Today we make you scream in laughter-pain, tomorrow we'll babysit your kids so you can have a date night." It's male bonding at its weirdest and finest.

Let's not forget the sheer spectacle: If you're a guest who didn't know this was coming, you might think the groomsmen completely lost their minds. One minute you're enjoying soju and karaoke, the next the groom is dangling upside-down like a caught fish himself, while his buddies play a percussive tune on his soles. If there were any evil spirits or bad juju, surely they've been scared off by this bizarre display.

In the pantheon of wedding traditions, the Korean foot-whipping is one that really keeps everyone on their toes – pun absolutely intended. It reminds us that not all ceremonies are solemn; some are downright slapstick (slap-fish?). And maybe there's a takeaway for all marriages: unexpected things will happen, sometimes you'll feel pain or embarrassment, but if you can laugh through it (as the groom is meant to do), you'll be just fine. Plus, it sets the precedent that the bride now owes the groom a really good foot rub later – fair is fair, right?

Cupid's Missed Arrows – In China's Yugur culture, the groom fires three headless arrows at his bride, then breaks them to seal eternal love

Our final stop on this whirlwind tour of "Wait, is this really a wedding or an episode of *Jackass*?" brings us to a lesser-known corner of China, home to the Yugur people. The Yugur have a tradition that sounds like a mashup of a fairy-tale romance and an archery contest. Picture this: a groom with a bow and arrow taking aim at his bride. (Insert gasp here.) Now, before you call in the SWAT team, note that the arrows are headless – no sharp points, just the shafts. He's not trying to recreate a William Tell stunt with an apple on her head; he's enacting a ritual of love. The groom shoots three of these blunt arrows straight at his beloved. Afterwards, he calmly walks over, picks up the arrows, and in a gesture as symbolic as it is dramatic, breaks each arrow in half. Consider those arrows Cupid's darts – fired and then snapped to signify that the bond is unbreakable and no other arrows (or loves) are needed. Aww, right? In a slightly aggressive, "I almost shot my wife" kind of way.

Let's unpack this, because it's a scene begging for both analysis and some lighthearted ribbing. On one hand, it's quite poetic: the act of shooting the arrows is like saying "I've hit my target – my heart is yours and yours is mine." Breaking them says "and now nothing can ever break us apart, not even these arrows, because I won't allow any hurt to come between us." It's a promise of eternal love and fidelity, acted out in a visually striking way. Beats a boring unity candle ceremony, if you ask me.

On the other hand… he's shooting arrows at his bride! Headless or not, that takes trust. I mean, what if his aim is off? I hope to heaven they remove *all* the sharp bits, because an arrow bouncing off your shoulder still smarts. Perhaps the bride wears a nice thick gown just in case. I'd love to know the conversation beforehand: "Honey, at the ceremony, I'm going to shoot some arrows at you." "Oh, of course dear. Should I wear the Kevlar-lined wedding dress or will taffeta do?" It's a tradition that must have started way back when grooms were adept hunters or warriors. Modern city-dwelling Yugur grooms might have to practice at the local archery range to not embarrass themselves. Last thing you want is to miss your bride completely and accidentally spear the wedding cake. Talk about Cupid's missed arrows!

This ritual is a field day for analogies. It's like a live-action Cupid scenario – Cupid usually aims for the heart, but our groom here literally takes aim at his bride to show his love. If you think proposals with flash mobs are elaborate, try finding a guy who declares love by armed projectile. It's also the only wedding tradition I know that doubles as a marksmanship exam. Maybe the bride's family watches closely: if he can land all three shots near her (but not *on* her – important nuance!), he's proven his worth as a protector and provider. If he's fumbling with the bow like a total newbie, well… maybe consider crossbow counseling or something.

For a contemporary spin, imagine the memes: a photo of a groom mid-draw with the caption "When you love her *so much* you'd shoot her (with love)." Or the bride telling her friends, "Yeah, he really swept me off my feet – by firing arrows at me. It was the most romantic thing ever, after I confirmed I wasn't bleeding." In terms of celebrity parallels, this is like if Katniss Everdeen married Hawkeye and incorporated their hobbies into the ceremony. Archery as romance. Legolas from *The Lord of the Rings* is somewhere nodding in approval. On the political satire front, can't you just see a cartoon where a politician is shooting arrows labeled "promises" at Lady Liberty or something? (Actually, let's leave politics out of this love story before it gets weird.)

Now, the arrow-breaking part deserves its own spotlight. It's the big finish – our groom snaps the arrows confidently, likely making a loud *crack*. This action says: no more arrows will ever be shot in this marriage. In other words, no infidelity (he won't direct Cupid's arrow at anyone else), and no harm shall come to the bride from him. It's like he's disarming himself. "I had the weapons, I used them in the name of love, and now I render them useless. I couldn't hurt you even if I wanted to – which I don't, ever." That's rather beautiful, in a macho, hero-of-the-village kind of way. It's the stuff of legend – I wouldn't be surprised if some epic folk song exists about a bridegroom's arrow ceremony.

Beyond the theatrics, what's the life lesson for the rest of us? It might be that love requires bold gestures and vulnerability. The bride literally stands there and lets her man shoot arrows at her – that's trust! She has faith that he will not harm her. In any marriage, that trust is key (though usually it's more about trusting your partner with finances or feelings, not physical projectiles, but hey, same principle). The groom, by breaking the arrows, is showing commitment: once this wedding is done, there's no turning back, no second-guessing. We break the "exit" options, so to speak. We're in it for the long haul, baby. It's kind of the opposite of having divorce on the table – he symbolically *removes the weapons* that could break the relationship. If every couple had that mindset (maybe sans weaponry), perhaps more marriages would go the distance.

And let's not overlook the sheer cool factor. Of all the rituals we've explored, this one might win for most cinematic. I mean, if I attended a wedding where a dude fired arrows across the stage at his bride and then snapped them, I'd be both mildly terrified and extremely impressed. It's giving major "end of an action-romance movie" vibes. Cue the slow clap as guests marvel at the display of love and archery.

So there we have it – from no-smile ceremonies to saliva blessings, from garbage showers to fish foot-whippings, and now arrow shooting. Who knew saying "I do" could involve so many strange mini-adventures? These outlandish rituals, as weird and *what the-heck* as they are, each carry a kernel of truth about marriage: it's serious, it's messy, it's painful, it requires humor and trust, and it's sealed with bold promises. Plus, they make for fantastic stories to tell at dinner parties.

In the end, whether or not you'd personally partake in any of these traditions (I'll pass on the fish pedicure, thanks), you've got to love the rich tapestry of human customs. They prove that love is universal, but the ways we celebrate it can be wonderfully diverse – and sometimes downright bizarre. One couple's "perfect day" might be another's "you did *what* at your wedding?!" And that's the beauty of it. So laugh, cringe, and learn a little from these outlandish rituals. After all, a marriage that starts with a headless arrow, a slimy hug from Dad, a garbage bath, a foot-thwacking, or an extreme poker face is bound to have a lifetime of great anecdotes – and perhaps that's the biggest lesson: marriage is the greatest adventure, no matter how you kick it off. Enjoy the ride, and watch out for flying fish and arrows along the way!

Chapter 3

The Party's Just Getting Weird – Strange Post-Wedding Customs

Y ou thought the ceremony was the crazy part? Oh no, my friend. That was just the opening act. Once the "I do" is done and the cake is cut, in some cultures the real fun begins. And by fun, I mean those *strange post-wedding customs* that will make your garter toss and drunken conga line look downright mundane. Buckle up—this party's just getting weird.

Toilet Bowl Cocktail – In an old French tradition, wedding guests mix leftover food and drink in a toilet and demand the newlyweds chug it

Let's kick things off in France, the land of fine wine, fine dining, and apparently toilet-bowl cocktails for the newlyweds. Oui, you read that correctly. Imagine you're blissfully exhausted after your wedding reception, ready to ride off into the sunset (or at least to the honeymoon suite), when suddenly your dear friends block the way, cackling like mischievous hyenas. In their hands: a porcelain toilet bowl. (Hopefully a *clean* one—pray it's a prop and not from the venue's actual restroom.) Floating inside this loo punch bowl is a concoction of leftover wedding cake, bits of baguette, backwash from half-finished champagne glasses, maybe some chocolate, and who knows what else from the buffet. It's the unholy lovechild of a frat house punch and a dumpster dive, served chilled. And guess who has to drink it? Oui, *monsieur et madame* Newlywed, that's who.

They call this charming tradition "La Soupe", presumably because "garbage stew" was too on-the-nose. The idea is that the couple needs a little extra *oomph* for their wedding night—some say it's meant to give them strength. (Honestly, a glass of Bordeaux and a wink would suffice, but hey, who am I to question centuries of French innovation?) Personally, I suspect this ritual was invented by some resentful bridesmaid who wanted payback for being forced to wear a taffeta dress. What better revenge than making the happy couple guzzle a witch's brew of party scraps from a toilet?

Now, if you're gagging a little at the thought, you're not alone. Picture the bride and groom at this moment: she's holding her nose; he's loosening his bow tie and trying not to recall the sight of Uncle Pierre's chewed escargot floating in the mix. Around them, their friends bang on pots and pans (because of course they add a marching-band vibe to this horror) and chant "Drink! Drink! Drink!" like it's a college kegger. This is essentially Fear Factor: Wedding Edition. Even the *Jackass* guys might think twice. But the newlyweds are good sports (they kind of have to be), so they grab the toilet-bowl chalice together and, in a show of true love—and iron stomachs—they chug. Maybe not the whole thing; let's hope tradition allows a few heroic sips to count. Either way, they'll definitely deserve a real drink after. *Champagne flute? Nah, just pass the mouthwash.*

If there's a silver lining (and we're really stretching for one here), it's that enduring this gross-out gauntlet as a team can only strengthen the couple's bond. Nothing says "we're in this together" like doing a shot of toilet sangria with your new spouse. It's basically a crash course in marriage: sometimes you have to swallow some nasty stuff and smile through it—figuratively, we hope. After surviving that, "til death do us part" doesn't seem so hard.

Three-Day Lockdown – Borneo's Tidong newlyweds can't leave their room or use the bathroom for 72 hours after the wedding

Moving on from toilets to the complete lack of toilets—allow me to introduce the Tidong community of Borneo, who clearly asked themselves, "How can we make newlyweds even more uncomfortable than drinking from a latrine?" The answer: lock them in a room for three days and forbid them from using the bathroom. Yes, you read that correctly. For 72 hours after the wedding, Tidong couples endure a bladder-busting honeymoon lockdown. No peeing, no pooping, no sneaking out for a quick Snickers bar—nada. It's just the two of them in matrimonial captivity, under the watchful eye of relatives who ensure they don't cheat and take a secret tinkle. (Imagine your sweet auntie acting as a prison warden, standing guard outside your door with the intensity of a Buckingham Palace guard, but with a much smaller bladder herself.)

Why, you ask, would anyone willingly subject lovebirds to this torturous game of "Hold It or Die Trying"? Well, the Tidong believe that this extreme test of endurance brings good luck, fertility, and a strong marriage. It's like a spiritual cleanse—literally *cleansing* their systems by not letting anything out. According to folklore, if the couple can tough it out together without any bathroom breaks, they'll be blessed with healthy babies and a lasting union. Break the rules, and it's bad news: everything from broken marriages to stillborn children. No pressure, right? (If you thought forgetting to feed your Tamagotchi in the '90s had dire consequences, try being responsible for not cursing your future offspring just because you *really* had to go number two.)

To help the newlyweds succeed (and not, you know, keel over from dehydration), friends and family put them on a strict regimen: minimal food and sip-sized drinks. Basically the opposite of a wedding reception buffet. The couple is essentially on the weirdest detox diet ever—green juice cleanse, meet bladder cleanse. And you better believe they're counting down every one of those 4,320 minutes. This is the ultimate new-marriage challenge: move over, Escape Room, the Tidong have the market cornered on confined-space teamwork. Forget the Newlywed Game; this is like the Newlywed Hunger Games. May the odds be ever in your favor, and may your bladder be of steel.

If there's a bright side (again, we're squinting here), it's that if a couple can survive this ordeal without one of them committing homicide, they're pretty much set to handle anything. Three-day road trip with a broken A/C? Piece of cake. Twin toddlers potty-training? Bring it on. Annoying in-laws dropping by unannounced? After Auntie stood guard outside your honeymoon suite listening for flushes, nothing can faze you. Consider it an extreme bonding experience. Some couples get matching tattoos to symbolize their unity; Tidong couples get matching kidney stress and a mutual agreement that the first stop after day three is the bathroom, *now*. Talk about starting a marriage with a true test of patience—literally holding it in for love.

The Kissing Commotion – In Sweden, if one newlywed leaves to use the restroom, the other gets mobbed with kisses by everyone left behind

After the no-kiss, no-bathroom situation in Borneo, Sweden might sound like a cakewalk. They *do* get bathroom breaks at Swedish weddings, but there's a catch—if a bride or groom dares to leave the room, their spouse is about to get mobbed with kisses by everyone left behind. Consider it a consolation prize for whoever's still at the table: "Sorry your honey had to go pee, here, have a smooch... or twenty."

Yes, in the progressive land of IKEA and ABBA, they have a tradition that's one part sweet and two parts chaos. The rule: whenever the groom leaves the reception (to answer nature's call or maybe finally take off those pinching dress shoes), all the gentlemen guests line up to plant a kiss on the bride. And when the bride slips away (perhaps to fix her lipstick), the lady guests get to rush over and give the groom a peck. The result? A sort of kissing flash mob where our poor newlywed is caught in a storm of affectionate assailants.

Now, imagine being the spouse under siege. One minute you're sipping champagne, the next you've got more strangers kissing you than a politician at a county fair. It's presumably just pecks on the cheek—though there's always that one prankster friend who aims a little too close to the lips. By the time your beloved returns, you look like you lost a fight with a lipstick dispenser. Welcome back, honey! Hope your bathroom break was refreshing, because I just got to first base with half the guests.

This tradition can be a real test of trust (and sense of humor). Jealous types, be warned: either hold your bladder or practice some Zen. Most couples roll with it, laughing as they wipe away the evidence. It's all in good fun—the wedding equivalent of a halftime show. Guests love it, too. There might even be a friendly competition over who got more kisses, the bride or groom. I can almost hear the best man taking bets.

In a way, it's weirdly sweet. It ensures the newlyweds are never lonely; they're literally showered with affection the second one of them is gone. It also encourages them to stick together like glue—because stepping away means leaving your love open to a swarm of eager smoochers. (I suspect some have mastered the art of synchronized bathroom breaks to avoid the onslaught.)

And let's not overlook the entertainment value. As a guest, how often do you get permission to smooch someone else's new spouse without getting punched? It's like a hall pass, but grandma-approved. In fact, Grandma might be first in line—don't underestimate the gleam in her eye. Honestly, this custom could spice up weddings elsewhere. Imagine a Hollywood wedding with this rule: if Beyoncé left Jay-Z alone for one minute, he'd get mobbed by the Single Ladies (cue the dance). The tabloids would explode.

In the end, the Swedish kissing commotion is a lighthearted reminder not to take things too seriously. Marriage will have its little separations and temptations, but a couple that can laugh through a storm of friendly kisses is probably going to do just fine. Plus, it makes for great photos. The bride blowing kisses like a movie star, the groom pretending to swoon under a pile of admirers—it's Instagram gold. Just maybe warn your out-of-town guests beforehand that *when nature calls, so do the kissers.*

Human Doormat – In the Marquesas Islands, relatives lie face-down so the bride and groom can literally walk on them as a post-ceremony sendoff

If you thought your family went out of their way to make your wedding day special, you haven't met the folks in the Marquesas Islands of French Polynesia. Here, relatives show their love and support by becoming the welcome mat for the newlyweds—literally. In a tradition that will make you simultaneously say "awww" and "WTF," the close family of the bride (and sometimes the groom) lie down on the ground, side by side, face-down, forming a human carpet. Then, as the couple leaves the ceremony, they walk *over* their loved ones. Yes, on top of them. Talk about *stepping into your new life together*—on the backs of your family.

Try to picture this without giggling: Mom, Dad, weird Uncle Tiko, and half-a-dozen cousins all in their finest island attire, willingly flopping onto the dirt like they're planking in 2010, so the bride and groom's fancy shoes don't touch the ground. The newlyweds gingerly tiptoe across this sea of bodies.

Now, before you label this the world's most extreme act of family self-sacrifice, consider the sentiment behind it. It's actually kind of sweet in a "we love you so much we'd lay down in the dirt for you" way. These relatives are basically saying, *we support you so strongly, we'll be the foundation you walk on.* Symbolism level 100, right? It gives *"I've got your back"* a whole new very tangible meaning. And you thought holding the bride's dress train was a big ask—try being the rug under her feet.

In fairness, this is probably more ceremonious than painful. They usually do it after the reception, when everyone's a little giddy (and maybe a tad tipsy on island rum). And it likely lasts only a few seconds—one slow, careful procession of the newlyweds walking across, then cheers and laughter as everyone gets up and brushes themselves off (probably checking for shoe prints on their nice clothes). Still, one hopes the couple are polite about it. This isn't the moment to channel your inner Godzilla and stomp around. Light footsteps, happy couple. These folks literally laid themselves down for you; the least you can do is not leave a stiletto mark on grandma's back.

For the marriage itself, the *human doormat* sends a clear message: remember who helped you get here (and who has the footprint-shaped bruises to prove it). It's a reminder to stay humble and grateful, even as you're literally placed above your elders for a moment. And likely it's a fun story that will be told at every anniversary: "Remember when cousin Pua volunteered as head of the carpet and ended up with a face full of sand? Good times." It might even become a bit of marital folklore—"We walked on people at our wedding, we can walk through any challenge!" If nothing else, the couple leaves their reception with a spring in their step—courtesy of stepping on Auntie's back—and a one-of-a-kind memory to start off their marriage.

In-Law Chaperones – In Swahili culture, a village elder or the bride's mother may escort the couple to the bedroom to "advise" the bride on the wedding night

As if our tour of bizarre post-wedding customs hasn't been awkward enough, we've saved the most *intimate* for last. Brace yourselves (and maybe clutch a pillow in sympathetic embarrassment), because in some Swahili communities, the newlyweds' first night together comes with… a chaperone. And not just any chaperone, but often a village elder or even the bride's own mother. I'll give you a moment to let that sink in. Yes, folks, your mother-in-law might literally join you on your wedding night to give pointers. If you're squirming now, imagine how the poor bride and groom feel.

Here's the setup: The wedding festivities are winding down, the couple is ushered to their bedroom, probably equal parts excited and nervous for the *big moment*. Suddenly, in walks Grandma or Mom or Auntie, who plants herself in a chair like she's about to watch a pay-per-view boxing match, except the only thing punching here will be… (no, let's not complete that analogy). The elder is there to "advise" the bride, which is a polite way of saying live tutorial. Maybe it starts with some gentle encouragement: "Don't be shy, dear, it's okay." Then perhaps a few technical pointers are offered. In the worst-case scenarios (avert your eyes), she might even demonstrate what the bride is supposed to do, right there, using whatever... props... are handy (let's hope not). The involvement could range from simple moral support to full-on TMI territory. As modern Western folks, it's hard to fathom anything beyond "moral support" being remotely okay, but culturally this is meant to be helpful and wise. Supposedly.

For the couple, maintaining a sense of humor (or sanity) is key. I imagine the groom lying there stiff as a board, trying to think unsexy thoughts (baseball? Grandma's knitting?) to keep his cool, while also keenly aware that his mother-in-law is *in the room*, grading his performance like an Olympic judge. The bride, mortified, endures Mom essentially giving a TED Talk titled *"Bedroom Basics: How to Please Your Spouse 101."* In any other context, this scenario would land you in therapy or on a cringe comedy sketch, but on that night, it's their reality.

Naturally, any outsider hearing this goes, "I would rather move to Mars than have my mom coach my sex life." But let's attempt to see the cultural perspective for a second: in communities where premarital sex is rare and sex education is, shall we say, minimal, this tradition evolved to ensure the bride knows what to expect and how to make the night a success. Think of it as training wheels for the wedding night, guided by someone who (as awkward as it is) has been around the block and genuinely wants the marriage to start off right.

If there's a lesson to squeeze out of this (besides the obvious "lock the door"), it's that marriage often involves family in weird ways. Setting boundaries with in-laws might as well start on day one—like, literally, "Mom, please leave the bedroom." It's a crash course in communicating uncomfortable truths to your new family. And if you can survive the embarrassment of Mom giving bedroom advice in person, you're pretty much bulletproof as a duo. Suddenly all those little newlywed embarrassments—morning bad breath, flubbed vows, that wardrobe malfunction—pale in comparison. Your threshold for awkward is now stratospherically high. Think of it as immunity through exposure: you've been vaccinated against mortifying family interference.

So to all the soon-to-be-newlyweds out there feeling nervous about the wedding night, take heart: at least you probably won't have a play-by-play commentator in the room. And if you do find yourself in a Swahili scenario with Grandma gearing up to chaperone, well, stock up on humor (and a sturdy lock). Thank her for the "help," and then kindly ask her to never do that again. In the most respectful way, of course—she *is* an elder, after all.

After this whirlwind tour of post-nuptial nuttiness, you might be thinking your own wedding (past or future) was pretty tame. Or maybe you're just grateful the wildest thing at your reception was Uncle Bob's off-key karaoke of "Sweet Caroline." Either way, these outrageous customs make for great stories about what people will do for love and luck.

Beneath the shock and laughter, each bizarre ritual hides a nugget of truth about marriage. It can be messy and require teamwork (raise a glass to toilet soup). It demands endurance and patience (maybe not three-days-no-bathroom patience, but close). It thrives on trust and letting go (if those Swedes can endure a smooch ambush, you can survive a night apart). It's propped up by family support (ideally without using relatives as rugs). And yes, a bit of wisdom from elders helps (preferably not delivered live on your honeymoon).

Perhaps it's universal: no matter how different our cultures are, we all love to haze newlyweds with a little absurdity and affection. Call it a playful initiation—balancing out all that attention and free cookware they got. Humans are nothing if not creative in celebrating love.

So here's to marriage and all its crazy, beautiful rituals. When it's your turn to tie the knot, skip the toilet cocktail and pop some champagne, skip the bladder marathon and take a bathroom break, and definitely skip having Mom as your bedroom coach. But carry forward the spirit behind these traditions: unity, resilience, trust, support, and most of all, a shared sense of humor. Because if marriage isn't at least a little bizarre and a lot of fun, you might be doing it wrong. Cheers—and please, drink from a normal glass!

Chapter 4

Till Death and Beyond – Ghosts, Corpses, and Otherworldly Unions

Imagine standing at the altar, heart pounding, ready to say "I do" – except your spouse-to-be is, well, *dead*. If you think "till death do us part" is supposed to be the end of the story, think again. Across time and cultures, people have found wildly creative loopholes to keep the wedding bells ringing even when one (or both) parties have shuffled off this mortal coil. Welcome to the bizarre bridal expo of the afterlife, where ghost grooms, corpse brides, and even divine husbands are all on the guest list. We're about to take a humorous honeymoon beyond the veil, exploring real customs that prove love (or at least marriage) can transcend not just cultures, but life and death itself. Buckle up – you're about to say "I do" to some seriously spooky nuptials.

Tomb-Mates – Ancient Chinese ghost weddings marry two deceased people (or even a living person to a dead one) so no soul travels lonely

Let's kick off our matrimonial tour six feet under – in ancient China, where being dead is hardly an excuse to stay single. Picture a traditional Chinese family ages ago: their dearly departed son has tragically died unwed. Rather than let him wander the afterlife as a lonely bachelor (how shameful!), the family sets out to find him a nice ghost bride. Yes, a *ghost* bride. They essentially plan a wedding for their late son because no soul should travel to the afterlife alone. It's like *The Bachelor*, except the bachelor is a literal ghost and the rose ceremony takes place at a gravesite.

These "ghost weddings" (minghun) have been part of Chinese tradition for millennia. And they come with all the usual wedding trappings – just with more incense and fewer heartbeats. Often, two deceased people are married to each other, joining them as a couple in the spirit world.

In some cases, a living person might even marry a dead person – the ultimate long-distance relationship. If a woman's fiancé died before the big day, she might still go through with the wedding post-mortem. Instead of a groom in a tux, she'll stand beside a symbolic stand-in (historically, sometimes a white rooster in place of the groom – and you thought your wedding was strange). She'd then live with his family as his widow. It's an extreme way to satisfy familial expectations – even death won't get you out of being married.

The practical side of these spooky unions usually came down to family duty and a dash of superstition. In traditional Chinese culture, an unmarried ghost could turn into a restless troublemaker. Ancestors want to see their kin settled down, even if the ceremony happens after one party is already in a coffin. It's morbidly sweet – a bit of spectral matchmaking to keep the ancestors happy. There were other motives too: maybe the family needed a daughter-in-law to honor the ancestors, or a posthumous son to carry on the family name. No son to carry on the name? Marry the departed off to a ghost bride and adopt an heir in their name. Tradition finds a way – even if it means doing paperwork at the cemetery.

Of course, even the afterlife has a market economy. The practice even sparked a macabre side hustle: people literally stole corpses to serve as "ghost brides." (Talk about digging up a date.) One moment you're resting in peace; next you're an unwitting newlywed in someone else's tomb.

So, what's married life like when one spouse is a ghost? On the bright side, ghost spouses don't leave wet towels on the bed or snore at night – bliss! On the other hand, try settling an argument via Ouija board. Good luck finding a marriage counselor for the living-dead divide.

In the end, ghost marriages show how far families will go to fulfill obligations. Next time your kin nag you to settle down, be grateful they're not literally digging up a date for you. Not even death was a valid excuse to dodge a wedding in this tradition.

The Ghost Groom – Among the Dinka and Nuer of South Sudan, a woman may marry a deceased man via his brother; children from the union are legally the dead man's heirs

If you thought ghost marriages were confined to ancient China, the afterlife has more up its sleeve. For our next stop, we're heading to South Sudan, where "till death do us part" gets a clever workaround. Meet the Dinka and Nuer peoples, who have their own spectral spin on matrimony. Here, it's all about the ghost groom – a marriage where the groom is dearly departed but still manages to have kids.

Imagine a young Nuer woman is set to marry a man named Bol, but – plot twist – Bol dies unexpectedly before the wedding. Bol's family, not about to let a perfectly good marriage arrangement go to waste, says, "You know what? Bol may be gone, but we promised him a wife. So you, dear, will marry Bol's ghost."

Bol's brother steps in as a stand-in for the ceremony and, ahem, for the wedding night too. Physically, the brother becomes the de facto husband, but spiritually and legally, everyone pretends (with a respectful wink) that Bol is the groom. Any children from this union are considered Bol's kids. Yep – ghost dad gets all the credit on the birth certificates, while the living brother is essentially the duty-bound surrogate. He's like a stunt double who does the hard work but doesn't get the Oscar – or in this case, the title of husband.

Why go to such lengths? As with Chinese ghost weddings, it's about family lineage and keeping spirits happy. In Dinka and Nuer culture, lineage and heirs are a huge deal – who's going to inherit the family cattle and carry on the name? If a man dies without children, it's a crisis. The ghost marriage fixes that: the deceased man "has" children posthumously, courtesy of his obliging brother and bride. It's a family plan in the most literal sense. On paper, those kids call the dead man "Father." They might even visit Dad's grave on Father's Day with a card – morbid, yet oddly heartwarming.

There's also a practical angle: taking care of the widow (or rather, the would-be widow). Instead of sending the would-be bride home, her in-laws keep her in the family and give her a substitute husband so she's provided for. You marry the family here, and if your husband checks out early, the family will literally provide a replacement. A compelling reason to be nice to your brothers-in-law!

Believe it or not, among the Nuer, ghost marriages used to be almost as common as regular marriages. Some women even saw advantages to a ghost husband. If she was wealthy and had property to her name, marrying a dead man meant she could retain control of her assets – no living husband around to claim her cattle or tell her what to do. Ghost groom isn't going to complain if she spends her own money. As unconventional life plans go, "marry a dead guy to stay independent" was surprisingly effective.

The ghost groom tradition gives us a rather wild marriage lesson: sometimes marriage is less about two lovebirds and more about the whole flock. It's marriage as a communal duty, a team sport that even death can't bench you from. The living brother's commitment to stand in for his spectral sibling reminds us that family can ask some pretty strange favors in the name of loyalty. It's bizarre and fascinating – and it makes planning a normal wedding with two living people feel like a piece of cake by comparison. At the very least, it puts a new spin on the phrase "over my dead body" – in South Sudan, that's just the beginning of the wedding plan.

Posthumous "I Do" – French law uniquely allows marrying a dead fiancé (with presidential approval), turning 'til death do us part on its head

So far we've mingled with ghosts and in-laws, but you might be thinking, "Surely in the modern world, no one's walking down the aisle with a corpse, right?" Ah, mes amis, bienvenue en France – leave it to the French, connoisseurs of romance *and* bureaucracy, to legalize l'amour beyond la mort. In France, you actually can marry your deceased fiancé. It's called posthumous marriage, and it's 100% legal (provided you fill out the paperwork, naturellement).

The custom dates back to 1959, when a dam burst in Fréjus and tragically killed hundreds, including a young man who was engaged to be married. His bereaved fiancée begged the government to let her finish the wedding plans, even though her groom was now, unfortunately, in the great beyond. In a move that sounds like it came from a French novel, the authorities (all the way up to the President himself) said *oui*. They passed a law allowing the marriage to go ahead if you can prove the wedding was already planned and death simply crashed the party. In practice, you need the President's personal approval to marry a dead person – basically, the ultimate permission slip.

A posthumous wedding in France is both poignant and a little surreal. The living bride or groom stands beside a photograph of their late partner during the ceremony. There's an empty space where the dearly departed would be, and the vows are spoken as if they were there (talk about "in spirit"). The officiant declares them married, the living party signs the register for two, and just like that, one of the spouses is legally wed and dead.

The marriage is retroactively dated to just before the death, so it's as if the wedding happened in the nick of time. Of course, it's largely symbolic – you won't get a partner to do the dishes or a surprise anniversary gift. It's truly love (and paperwork) for love's sake.

It's hard not to marvel at the mix of passion and red tape. Can you picture being so devoted (or perhaps so stubborn) that you're willing to stand in City Hall and say "I do" to thin air while clutching a presidential decree? On one hand, it's heartbreakingly romantic – the ultimate act of devotion beyond death. On the other, it's absurd. "Oh, you postponed your wedding because of rain? How cute. I went through with mine even though the groom was, shall we say, unavailable."

This custom turns the usual wedding vow on its head. Instead of "till death do us part," it's more like "death is just a minor inconvenience." It adds new meaning to cold feet at the altar – the absent spouse has cold *everything*. Yet, for those who choose this path, it's no joke but a deeply heartfelt gesture. It grants a sense of closure and honor: the idea that death might have taken your love, but it won't cheat you out of the wedding day you both wanted.

Naturally, a posthumous marriage raises some logistical questions (the French typically handle it with quiet dignity – but one can't help imagining a macabre comedy sketch about dancing with a portrait). Ultimately, the fact that this is even possible is a testament to French romanticism (and their love of official stamps and forms).

The life-and-death lesson here? Love sometimes means going the extra mile – even if that mile is straight into a cemetery with a pen and an officiant. It shows that in at least one corner of the world, true love transcends all, even the grave, with a little help from the law. For the rest of us, it certainly puts commitment into perspective – at least you don't need a presidential seal of approval to marry your sweetheart.

Brotherly Backup – The ancient levirate custom required a widowed woman to marry her late husband's brother to keep it in the family (literally)

We've seen ghosts and bureaucrats play matchmaker; now we turn to an age-old custom that's all in the family. If you thought marrying a dead person was awkward, how about being required to marry your brother-in-law? This is the ancient tradition of levirate marriage –

humanity's original "backup husband" plan. This one goes way back, popping up in the Bible and in cultures from Africa to Asia. The premise was simple (and a tad uncomfortable): if a married man died without children, his widow was expected to marry his brother. It was the classic in-law duty – one brother steps out, another steps in, ring at the ready.

Imagine: you're mourning your husband, and before the grave dirt settles, your in-laws show up with your brother-in-law in tow, saying, "Don't worry, you two are getting hitched next Tuesday." For the widow, this could be somewhat okay (if she secretly found the brother-in-law kinda cute) or utterly horrifying (if he's the family weirdo). For the brother, it's a dutiful leap – maybe he had other plans, but family comes first.

The reasoning behind levirate marriage was to keep the family name and property alive. The first son born from the new union would legally be considered the child of the late husband, preserving his lineage. It also kept that dowry or land in-house. Think of it as a kind of social security for the widow and a lineage insurance policy for the family. There was even a famous biblical case: a man named Onan didn't exactly embrace this task with enthusiasm (long story short, he *really* botched the job), and according to the Bible, he was struck down for it. Message received: fulfill your brotherly duty, or else. Talk about pressure from above!

By modern standards, the whole thing is cringe-inducing. Widows as inheritance? Brother-in-law as consolation prize? Hard pass. But back then, it was a pragmatic solution in a world without pensions or life insurance. A widow without a child or a new husband could be left destitute. The levirate custom was the community's way of taking care of her – albeit in a manner that also conveniently kept everything in the family. It also reinforced that when you marry someone, you really marry the whole family (fine print and all).

The lesson from the levirate custom? Marriage hasn't always been about starry-eyed lovers; often it was about duty, continuity, and clan. It makes us appreciate living in a time when "keep it in the family" is more a joke about sharing Netflix passwords than sharing spouses. And be thankful that when we say "I do" today, the only person obligated is the one standing next to us – not his brother.

Holy Spouse – Nuns became "Brides of Christ," taking lifelong vows to marry God (complete with wedding rings and irreverent bridal metaphors in ceremony)

At this point, we've paired off humans with ghosts, dead fiancés, and brothers-in-law. Where to next? How about straight to heaven. Our final stop involves a groom who is omnipresent, omniscient, and isn't exactly available for dinner dates. We're talking about nuns – women who become "Brides of Christ." And no, that's not just a cute metaphor; in many orders, a nun's initiation can look a lot like a wedding ceremony. Vows? Check. Ring? Check. Lifelong commitment? Oh yeah. The only thing missing is the actual groom (unless you count a stained-glass Jesus in attendance).

When a woman takes her final vows to become a nun, the church often styles it in bridal terms. The new nun might wear a white veil or even a bridal gown. She lies face-down on the altar floor in a gesture of total devotion (picture a bride fainting at the altar – but in a holy way). She then professes vows of chastity and obedience, essentially swearing off all other potential husbands for the sake of one very divine spouse. As a token of this covenant, she often receives a ring – yes, a wedding ring – symbolizing that she is now wed to Jesus Christ.

They even call it a "mystical marriage." It's essentially official: Sister is a missus, and her husband is the Lord.

Of course, this marriage is purely spiritual. It's not like Christ will take out the convent trash or argue over the remote (an omniscient partner would win every argument by default). This is a union of devotion, meaning the nun dedicates all her love and service to her faith. It's quite beautiful in a deeply devout way. But with a dash of humor, there are some funny implications. For one, God ends up with an enormous number of brides. If there were a cosmic polygamy reality show, He'd be the star.

Being a Bride of Christ means the usual trappings of marriage take a backseat. There's no fancy honeymoon – more like a lifetime of service and prayer. No joint checking account squabbles either, thanks to that vow of poverty. And Valentine's Day? The best gift on offer is eternal salvation, which sure beats a dozen roses. It's the ultimate long-distance relationship, too – marrying someone who is always "out of town on business" (business being, you know, running the universe).

All joking aside, many nuns genuinely describe themselves as joyfully wed to Christ. They'll tell you they aren't single at all – they're spoken for by the Big Guy upstairs. And if anyone asks when you'll get married, well, you've got the ultimate mic-drop answer: "I'm married to God."

Ultimately, these otherworldly unions show that people will go to astonishing lengths for love, duty, or faith – even defying common sense (and mortality) in the process. From ghosts to God, the spectrum of matrimony is far wider and weirder than anything in a typical chapel. After hearing about folks marrying spirits and saints, your cousin's Elvis-officiated Vegas wedding seems downright ordinary. In the grand theater of marriage, there truly is someone for everyone – even if that someone is invisible. So here's to love, in all its bizarre beyond-the-grave glory. When some people say "forever," they really mean it.

Chapter 5

Two's Company, Ten's a Crowd – Unconventional Marriage Arrangements

Solomon's 700 Club – Biblical King Solomon had 700 wives and 300 concubines, a harem so famous it's recorded in scripture

When it comes to marriage, most people draw the line at one spouse. King Solomon of Israel must have missed that memo. This biblical king decided if one wife is good, 700 might be better – and for good measure he threw in 300 concubines on the side. Yes, you read that right: 700 wives and 300 concubines. That's one thousand women in his official romantic circle. Talk about the ultimate "friends and family" plan! His harem was so legendary it got a shout-out in the Old Testament, as if to say, *"This guy's love life is one for the ages."*

Solomon was famed for his wisdom, but one has to wonder how wise it is to have a spouse for every day of the year (with a few hundred spares). Sure, he authored Proverbs and could solve a dispute between two mothers with a sword trick, but could he remember all his wives' names? Imagine the nightly roll call at the dinner table: "Dearest Wife #142… are you present? And where's Concubine #56? I haven't seen her since last Passover." Even the great Solomon might have occasionally resorted to a generic "Oh, uh… sweetie." When in doubt, *sweetie* covers all bases.

How does one end up with 700 wives? In Solomon's case, it helped to be a king sealing alliances. Marrying princesses was the diplomatic email of the day – You've got a new wife! Each royal marriage was a political alliance, adding another foreign princess to his collection. Moabites, Ammonites, Hittites – Solomon was an equal-opportunity husband if it meant more peace treaties (and maybe a new cuisine at the palace potluck). Of course, with that many in-laws, palace life probably got intense. No wonder one proverb in the Bible sighs that "better to live on a roof than share a house with a quarrelsome wife." Multiply that scenario by 700 and you understand the sentiment.

There were consequences beyond needing a spreadsheet for anniversaries. The story goes that Solomon's wives eventually "turned his heart" away from his own traditions. Hard not to pick up a few new hobbies or deities when you have a thousand partners suggesting, "Honey, have you considered worshipping *my* gods this weekend?" If one wife can nag you to take out the trash, imagine a thousand voices pushing their own honey-do lists and holy days. Even the wisest man could end up spiritually exhausted and chronically outvoted.

In modern terms, Solomon's matrimonial excess makes celebrity playboys look like monks. Elizabeth Taylor had eight husbands? Please. If reality TV existed in 950 BC, we'd be watching *The Real Housewives of Jerusalem* – with a cast of hundreds and drama that makes *Game of Thrones* look like a kiddie show. The season finale would be Solomon frantically trying to gift each wife something special without mixing them up (spoiler: he'd need 700 personalized coffee mugs).

Marriage lesson: Quality over quantity, folks. Love may be boundless, but your attention span isn't. Solomon's thousand-strong spouse club is a biblical cautionary tale that sometimes more is just more headache. Better to cherish one partner than lose track of hundreds.

Brother-Husbands – In rural Tibet, fraternal polyandry lets one wife marry multiple brothers to keep family property intact

If Solomon was hoarding wives, here's a twist: one wife with multiple husbands – who just so happen to be each other's brothers. In the highlands of rural Tibet, this is a traditional practice called fraternal polyandry. One woman marries a set of brothers, and they all share one wife under one roof. Picture a wedding where the bride walks down the aisle and finds not one groom, but a whole lineup of brothers in matching outfits. (Buy one dowry, get several husbands free!)

Why do this? The answer is practical: property. In these remote mountain regions, good farmland is scarce and family assets are precious. Rather than split the farm among all the sons (leaving everyone with a sad little plot), the brothers join forces by marrying the same woman and staying in one household. The family land stays intact and all the bros pool their labor. It's like a cooperative marriage: more hands to herd the yaks and fewer rival estates next door. Think of it as the ultimate family savings plan – with a very unorthodox joint checking account.

So how does daily life work with brother-husbands? Surprisingly, pretty smoothly (according to them, anyway). Usually the oldest brother is the household head, but all brothers are equal partners in the marriage after the "I do, I do, I do" has been said. They divvy up chores and take turns spending time with their shared wife, likely on a schedule as precise as a Swiss watch.

The wife treats all husbands the same – no favorites, because nothing wrecks brotherly bonds like "why does he get extra dumplings at dinner?"

Any children call all the brothers "father." There's no paternity testing or "that's your kid, this is mine" – it's one big happy family with multiple dads. In a way, the children have a whole tag team of fathers to coach soccer or help with homework.

To outsiders, this might sound like reality TV gold – *Sister Wives* in reverse. You can almost hear a producer pitching *Brother-Husbands of the Himalayas.*

But in these communities, it's normal life. Sure, there could be a tinge of jealousy now and then (siblings have rivalries, after all). Maybe Brother-Husband #2 gets annoyed when #3 hogs the conversation, or they argue over who gets the warm spot by the fire. Yet they're raised with the idea that teamwork and family unity come first. It's a family business, and all the husbands are on the management team, so they tend to work it out.

For the wife, having multiple husbands means having backup. If one husband is away trading in the valley, another is home repairing the roof, and another is watching the kids. It's built-in redundancy – kind of nice when you think about it. And the brothers? They've shared everything since childhood, so sharing a spouse is just taking "sharing is caring" to the extreme.

Marriage lesson: Family comes in all shapes and sizes. This tradition shows that when everyone's on the same page, even an unconventional setup can run like a (mostly) well-oiled machine. Cooperation and communication are key in any marriage arrangement – be it a one-woman-multiple-husbands setup or just a regular household figuring out who takes out the trash.

Free Love Commune – The 19th-century Oneida Community in New York practiced "complex marriage" where every man was married to every woman and vice versa

Fast forward to 19th-century New York, where a group of idealists decided to give conventional marriage the boot and try something wildly unorthodox: complex marriage. The Oneida Community, founded in 1848, believed that exclusive pair-bonding was old-fashioned selfishness. Why have just one spouse when you could, in a sense, be married to *everyone* in your community? In their free-love utopia, every man was considered married to every woman, and vice versa. Monogamy was out; a sort of holy group marriage was in. If this sounds like a recipe for drama, well, it was — but the Oneidans truly thought they were onto a heavenly idea. They basically turned their commune into a giant extended family where "Will you marry me?" became "Will you marry... all of us?"

In practice, complex marriage meant that any consenting adults in the community could pair up, often facilitated by a committee to make sure matches were *balanced*. (Yes, they had bureaucratic matchmaking – leave it to earnest Victorians to put formality into free love.)

Jealousy was treated as a personal failing to overcome. Exclusivity was a no-no; if you started giving one person extra attention, you'd get a gentle talking-to about being too "sticky" in your love. They wanted everybody to share everybody, like one big happy (if occasionally awkward) family.

Even children were communal. Babies were typically separated from their birth parents after weaning and raised in a group nursery so they'd view the community, not just Mom and Dad, as family. It's the ultimate "it takes a village" approach — Oneida took it literally. Parents might have a favorite rocking chair in the nursery, but they didn't tuck in the same kid every night. Imagine growing up with dozens of siblings and a rotating cast of parental figures doing bedtime stories. On the plus side, lots of love to go around; on the minus side, try figuring out who to make a Father's Day card for.

A charismatic fellow named John Humphrey Noyes led the community. He believed humans could achieve spiritual perfection, and apparently part of perfection involved an open marriage with 300 people. Under Noyes's guidance, Oneidans even tried a breeding program they dubbed stirpiculture – basically pairing up "ideal" community members to produce uber-babies. (If that sounds a bit eugenics-y, yes, it was. They were utopians *and* control freaks, it turns out.)

But their grand experiment in love sharing lasted surprisingly long – about 32 years – and by most accounts the community was industrious and relatively harmonious for a while. They ran a successful business making animal traps, and later, silverware. (Indeed, the fine Oneida flatware that might grace your dinner table came from these free-lovers. From swapping partners to spoons – life is full of twists.)

Eventually, human nature and outside pressure caught up with Oneida. Younger members started chafing at the strict rules, and the wider world looked on with scandalized eyes (and occasionally arrest warrants). In 1879, facing internal dissent and legal threats, Noyes fled to Canada, effectively ending the complex marriage system. The community morphed into a regular joint-stock company, focused on manufacturing silverware and living like more conventional folks. Oneida's wild ride was over, but it left behind a legacy as one of history's most peculiar social experiments.

Marriage lesson: Love is a beautiful thing – but maybe it works best when it's not trying to love *everyone at once*. The Oneida story shows that relationships can be as complex as you make them. Some ideals sound great in theory ("let's all share!") but turn out messy in practice (because feelings, unsurprisingly, aren't so easily regulated). On the bright side, even if communal marriage failed, we got some nice forks and knives out of the deal.

Nero's Nuptial Shenanigans – Roman Emperor Nero twice married men: taking one as his husband and later wedding a castrated boy as his wife in full imperial wedding pomp

Just when you think you've heard it all, let's visit ancient Rome for a true tale of marital absurdity. Roman Emperor **Nero** (first-century troublemaker extraordinaire) managed to turn the institution of marriage into a personal stage for scandal. How? By marrying not one but two different males in grand ceremonies, taking on roles as both bride *and* groom (at different times, of course – even Nero didn't try to be both in one go).

The first escapade: Nero "married" a male freedman named Pythagoras (no, not the triangle guy). During the festival of Saturnalia – when Romans were already in party mode – Nero decided to one-up everyone's revelry. He put on a bridal veil, decked himself out as the blushing bride, and wed Pythagoras in front of guests. Yes, the emperor **was** the bride. You can imagine the jaws on the floor in that wedding hall.

The Roman elite had seen depravity, but their ruler playing princess must have been a new peak (or valley). Senators in togas probably clapped dutifully, while internally whispering, "What in Jupiter's name is happening?"

Nero wasn't done. A while later, he took a fancy to a beautiful adolescent boy named Sporus, who apparently reminded him of his late wife Poppaea (whom Nero had conveniently removed from the picture via a violent tantrum). To make this union extra weird, Nero had Sporus castrated – effectively making the boy a eunuch – and then married him in a full imperial wedding ceremony.

This time Nero donned the groom's toga, and Sporus was dressed as a traditional Roman bride, complete with veil and dowry. They even held a public ceremony with all the usual pomp and feasting, as if this were the most normal thing ever. The citizens of Rome were treated to the spectacle of their crazed emperor parading his new "Empress" Sporus through the streets in a golden carriage, while Nero cooed and bestowed kisses like a proud newlywed.

Now, Romans weren't exactly prudish – this was a culture that worshipped gods with pretty wild love lives of their own. But Nero's nuptial shenanigans were off-the-charts bizarre even for Rome. To marry a man was unheard of; to publicly wed a castrated boy and call him *wife* was beyond scandalous. Yet who was going to tell Nero "no"? The man literally had legions at his command. So the Empire collectively gulped, gossiped behind closed doors, and went along with the charade.

For a modern perspective, imagine a world leader today announcing on live TV, "Surprise! I've taken a husband, and next week I'll be marrying a teenager as my wife – state banquet to follow." The world would lose its mind. But Nero did it and expected a parade. His story doesn't end in happily-ever-after (more like exile, suicide, and a footnote of infamy), but his marital choices definitely carved him a spot in the Bizarre Weddings Hall of Fame.

Marriage lesson: Just because you can do something doesn't mean you should. Marriage is supposed to involve love and mutual respect – not abduction, mutilation, and a hefty dose of delusion. Nero's tale is a reminder that power can make people do truly crazy things, but it doesn't make those things right. Let's keep wedding vows sincere and leave the imperial theatrics in the history books, shall we?

World's Largest Family – Indian polygamist Ziona Chana left behind 39 wives and 94 children, running a household of 167 people under one roof

For our final stop, meet a man who took "big family" to a whole new level. Ziona Chana of India (who passed away in 2021) was the proud patriarch of what's often called the world's largest family. We're talking

39 wives, 94 children, and 33 grandchildren, all living together as one gigantic clan. That's 167 people under one roof, with Ziona at the head of the dinner table. If you struggle to manage a family of four, imagine a family photo that needs a drone to fit everyone in frame.

Ziona's home in Mizoram state was a four-story building with about 100 rooms – basically an apartment block for his extended household. The daily routine ran like a well-drilled operation. His wives took turns in the kitchen, cooking monumental meals: think 200 pounds of rice and dozens of chickens just for dinner. The kids (and there were almost a hundred of them) had chores delegated, the older ones helping care for the younger. They essentially had their own little community – a private village where "Dad" was also the mayor, head chef, and principal of the home school.

How does one acquire 39 wives? Ziona led a local religious sect that permits polygamy, so he had the green light to marry to his heart's content.

And marry he did – reportedly even wedding ten women in a single year at one point. (Most people space out their marriages; Ziona treated it like a marathon with the occasional sprint.)

Most new wives joined when they were very young (by arrangement), and the family just kept expanding. Remarkably, the sister-wives got along and managed the household cooperatively. Living in one house, they operated on a schedule and maintained harmony – or as close to harmony as you can get with dozens of kids crying, laughing, and playing all at once.

Culturally, Ziona's family was a curiosity and even a tourist draw. People would travel to see this real-life mega-marriage in action, a *Big*

Love situation on steroids. It made reality TV polygamists like the cast of *Sister Wives* or the Duggar family (with their measly 19 kids) look positively quaint. Ziona himself seemed proud of his brood; he claimed to feel like a lucky man, blessed with so many to care for him in his old age. And one thing's for sure: forget remembering anniversaries – just learning all 167 names must have been a feat of memory worthy of its own Guinness World Record.

Marriage lesson: The phrase "the more, the merrier" has its limits. A huge family can be full of love and teamwork, but for most of us, managing one partner and a handful of kids is challenge enough. Ziona's story shows that with structure and commitment, even wild arrangements can function – but unless you have a 100-room house and saint-like patience, it's probably best not to try this at home.

Chapter 6

Headaches and Headless Exes – Royal Breakups in History

Breakups are hard. Breakups when you're wearing a crown? They're the stuff of legend – and not the good kind. In the royal world, a lover's quarrel can shake empires, spawn new religions, or literally cost someone their head. In this chapter, we're diving into some of the most bizarre royal breakups in history. We'll meet kings and queens whose "happily ever after" veered wildly off script – with results ranging from darkly hilarious to just plain horrific. Don't worry, we'll keep things light (and a bit irreverent) as we journey through these tales of marital woe. After all, if you can't laugh about Henry VIII's love life, you'd cry – and nobody wants tear-stained velvet in the Tudor court.

So grab some popcorn (and maybe a prenup), and let's witness five cases of noble nuptials that went terribly, gloriously wrong. From a king who changed the course of religion for a divorce, to queens who upgraded husbands like smartphones, to modern monarchs proving even fairy-tales can fracture – these stories offer timeless lessons in love, power, and why you should never underestimate a spouse with a plan. Enjoy the ride, and remember: Always keep your head in a breakup – especially if you're married to a Tudor.

1. The Divorce Heard 'Round the Church – England's Henry VIII split from the Catholic Church (and Catherine of Aragon) when the Pope refused his divorce

Let's start with the *mother of all royal breakups*: King Henry VIII versus Catherine of Aragon, with the Pope as an unwelcome marriage counselor. For two decades, Catherine was Henry's devoted Spanish queen. But their royal résumé lacked one crucial line item – a male heir. Catherine gave Henry a daughter (the future Mary I) and several stillborn or short-lived sons. Henry, desperate for a boy and smitten by a younger lady-in-waiting (the ambitious Anne Boleyn), decided his marriage was beyond repair.

In 1527, Henry asked Pope Clement VII for an annulment – basically, a royal "Can I speak to your manager?" moment. Henry argued that since Catherine had been briefly married to his late brother, their union was cursed in God's eyes. The Pope, under pressure from Catherine's powerful nephew (Holy Roman Emperor Charles V), stalled and ultimately said "no dice." The Catholic Church forbade divorce, and not even a king's whining could change that – or so the Pope thought.

Henry's response? Fine, I'll do it myself. If the Pope wouldn't grant a divorce, Henry would chuck the Pope's authority altogether. In 1534, he broke England away from Rome in a move that was equal parts petty and revolutionary. He declared himself head of a brand-new Church of England (because why not start your own religion to win an argument?). Conveniently, his new church was happy to grant the annulment. Catherine was out, Anne Boleyn was in, and by 1533 a very pregnant Anne was crowned Queen of England.

This breakup reverberated far beyond the royal bedroom. Henry's personal spat launched the English Reformation – basically England telling the Catholic Church, "It's not me, it's you." Monasteries were shut down, church lands snatched up, and centuries of religious tradition got a makeover, all because one stubborn husband wanted to swap wives. Catherine of Aragon spent her final years exiled from court (still defiantly calling herself the true queen till the end), and the Pope probably needed a stiff drink or two. The "divorce heard 'round the church" changed history in a way no one saw coming.

- **Marriage Lesson:** If the Pope says "no" to your divorce, just start your own church and say "yes" to yourself. Go big or go home (and take the country with you).

- **Takeaway:** Only a king with an ego the size of England would change his nation's religion to get rid of his wife. For everyone else: maybe try counseling *before* founding a new faith.

2. Annulment by Axe – When Anne Boleyn didn't produce a male heir, Henry VIII solved the "divorce" by beheading her – talk about an extreme breakup

You'd think after all the trouble Henry VIII went through to marry Anne Boleyn; he'd give her some slack. Nope. Henry's patience with wives was about as short as Anne's neck was soon to be. Anne did give Henry one healthy baby – but it was a *girl*, the future Elizabeth I. (In hindsight, a pretty awesome kid, but Henry wanted a boy and wasn't the type to appreciate irony.) Anne also had a couple of miscarriages, which only deepened Henry's royal sulk. Soon his eye wandered to Jane Seymour, a meek lady-in-waiting in Anne's entourage. We've got a pattern: once again, the king's current wife wasn't delivering a male heir, and the next woman in line looked awfully appealing.

In 1536, rather than amicably separate (an unheard-of concept for Tudor royals), Henry decided to solve his Anne problem with an executioner. He accused his queen of adultery, treason, and pretty much anything else that would stick – even outrageous stuff like incest with her brother. These charges were about as believable as dragon sightings, but that didn't matter. Anne was hauled off to the Tower of London, put on trial by a jury of nobles (many of whom either feared the king or hated Anne's guts), and convicted with lightning speed.

On May 19, 1536, Anne Boleyn met her tragic end. To her credit, she maintained her poise – even cracking a macabre joke about her "little neck" while awaiting the sword. A skilled French swordsman was brought in to ensure the deed was quick (if you're going to break up *that* hard, at least make it snappy). One swing, and Queen Anne went from Henry's wife to history.

Henry wasted no time mourning – in fact, he was betrothed to Jane Seymour the *next day*. By the following week and a half, he had a new wife. That's right: Henry's idea of closure was planning his next wedding before the blood on the chopping block was dry. Talk about moving on.

Anne's death stands as perhaps the most brutal royal breakup ever. It's one thing to split the estate or argue over who gets the dog; it's another to literally behead your spouse. Being Henry's queen was a lethal position – the Tudor version of a high-turnover job with deadly severance. The bitter twist? The daughter Anne left behind, Elizabeth, would go on to become one of England's greatest monarchs, outshining all of Daddy's precious sons. Henry's extreme breakup solved nothing in the long run, except rid him of a wife who dared to have a mind of her own.

- **Marriage Lesson:** "Till death do us part" is supposed to be poetic, not a to-do list. If your spouse treats the vow as an exit strategy, you might want to skip date night (and run for your life).

- **Takeaway:** Henry VIII's idea of an annulment was an axe. For the rest of us, this sets the bar of "worst breakup ever" so high (or low) that no amount of crazy ex drama today can quite compare.

3. Queen Upgrades – Eleanor of Aquitaine annulled her marriage to Louis VII of France on convenient consanguinity grounds, then promptly married a younger, future king

Not all royal breakups involve violent decapitation or schismatic chaos. Some are sly, calculated, and downright savvy. For a prime example, meet Eleanor of Aquitaine – the only woman to have been Queen of France *and* Queen of England, and the 12th century's answer to a powerhouse divorcee who wasn't about to let a little thing like "no divorce in Catholicism" stop her from upgrading her marriage.

Eleanor married King Louis VII of France in 1137, when they were both teenagers and not exactly a match made in heaven. She was bold, worldly, and owned half of what is now France (Aquitaine was *hers* – a vast duchy of wine, culture, and troublemakers). Louis VII, on the other hand, was pious, reserved, and reportedly more interested in praying than – ahem – playing. Opposites attract at first, but after 15 years, a couple of daughters, and one ill-fated joint trip on the Second Crusade (marriage road-trip from hell, anyone?), the royal pair realized they were about as compatible as a rock star and a monk.

But here's the kicker: in medieval Catholic Europe, divorce wasn't just frowned upon; it was basically nonexistent. You could get an annulment – but only if you could prove your marriage should never have happened in the first place. (It's like saying "Oops, we never *actually* were married, technical glitch!") Luckily for Eleanor, she and Louis had a trump card: they were technically *cousins*. Distant cousins, mind you – but close enough for Church law. In 1152, citing the ever-popular "consanguinity" (a fancy word for "we're too closely related"), the Church granted them an annulment. Boom – marriage erased. (The two daughters were declared legitimate but stayed in France with Dad, proving that custody arrangements have been a royal pain for centuries.)

Eleanor didn't spend one minute longer single than she had to. Barely eight weeks after the annulment, she shocked everyone by marrying a strapping 19-year-old named Henry – the future Henry II of England. Yes, our gal Eleanor essentially said, "Louis, it's not me, it's you (and our unfortunate genetic closeness). No hard feelings, but I've met this younger English guy and he's going places – specifically, to the English throne, and I'm hitching a ride." Talk about a rebound – or rather, an *upgrade*. Louis was in his mid-30s, Eleanor was around 30, and Henry was 19. In modern terms, this was a high-profile cougar move, and the medieval paparazzi (okay, chroniclers and gossips) were shook.

Marrying Henry turned out to be a game-changer. Eleanor brought her huge lands with her, so suddenly half of France belonged to the English crown – *awkward* for Louis. It also cemented Eleanor's legend as a fiercely independent woman. How many medieval queens can you name who basically said "I'm bored with this marriage, let's hit CTRL-Z and undo it"? The consanguinity excuse was a godsend – a ready-made "It's not *our* fault, we were related!" cover story for a very political breakup. Louis VII went on to marry again and finally got his long-awaited son (future King Philip II), so he was happy. And Eleanor? She had eight children with Henry II (including Richard the Lionheart and King John), and if Henry gave her trouble later, well, she gave back as good as she got (she even supported her sons in rebelling against him – the medieval equivalent of changing the locks).

As royal separations go, Eleanor's annulment was *relatively* civil: no war, no public executions, just some paperwork citing "irreconcilable cousinship." It shows that even in an age of arranged marriages and strict religious rules, a determined queen could work the system to her advantage. She's proof that sometimes the best way to get out of a bad marriage is to play by the rules in unexpected ways – and maybe trade up while you're at it.

- **Marriage Lesson:** When life (or the Church) hands you consanguinity, make annulment-ade. In other words, if you need out and there's a handy loophole (like "oops, we're cousins!"), use it shamelessly.

- **Takeaway:** A queen's gotta do what a queen's gotta do. Trading up your king is fair game if the first one turns out to be a bore – just double-check the family tree before your next wedding invite goes out.

4. No Divorce, No Problem – For centuries in Catholic Europe, clever nobles sought annulments (or exile to convents) to escape marriages, since divorce was off the table

Eleanor wasn't the only clever aristocrat to exploit the **no-divorce workaround**. For hundreds of years, in staunchly Catholic Europe, unhappy spouses had to get creative – or stay miserably married (with perhaps a discreet poisoning here or there, but we'll stick to the legal methods). Since the Church said "*'Til death do you part* and we mean it," enterprising nobles came up with some truly innovative exit strategies for doomed marriages. Desperate times, meet desperate measures.

The most popular strategy was what we just saw: find a flaw in the fine print. Medieval marriage was full of terms and conditions that nobody read until something went wrong. Need out? Suddenly everyone's poring over the rulebook looking for a loophole. Consanguinity (being related) was the all-time favorite. Didn't realize you and your spouse shared a great-great-grandpa? Well, shucks – clearly the marriage is invalid! Annulment granted; have a nice life. Fraud, coercion, insanity, a prior secret marriage – any "impediment" would do, if you could make it stick. The idea was to convince a Church court that the marriage never *truly* existed. And if you had money and influence, that wasn't too hard. (Bribing a bishop could work wonders – divine enlightenment sometimes needed a little cash incentive.)

Speaking of creative excuses: impotence and non-consummation were frequent flyers on the annulment scene. These led to some bizarre courtroom dramas. In one notorious "bedroom trial," a husband had to perform in bed with his wife while a group of elder women watched – to verify whether he could, uh, *perform* or not. (Nothing like an audience of grandmas to spice up the romance.) Predictably, the poor guy failed to rise to the occasion, the court declared the marriage unconsummated, and *poof* – no more marriage. It was humiliating, but effective. Think of it as the original reality show: *America's Got No Bedroom Talent* (the loser gets to be single again).

If concocting an annulment wasn't possible, there was always the convent strategy – essentially the "send your spouse to Jesus" plan. Noblemen who really wanted out might pressure their wives to take the veil and enter a convent, permanently removing them from the marriage. It wasn't a divorce, oh no – simply a wife pursuing a holy vocation (wink, wink). Once a woman became a nun, the marriage was effectively over (God became the husband, and He's not big on sharing). Some wives chose this escape willingly – a tranquil convent life could beat being chained to a lout. Others had it forced upon them, shipped off to an abbey against their will. Morally dubious? Absolutely. But it got the job done without cutting any heads off or incurring lightning bolts from heaven (usually).

Royal and noble history is filled with cases of "creative separation." King Louis XII of France, for example, claimed he'd been *forced* to marry his wife and that he was unable to consummate the union – conveniently clearing the way to dump her and wed someone else. (He even swore he was only impotent *with her* – a line only a king could get away with. The Pope granted the annulment, and Louis promptly proved his virility by fathering kids with wife #2. His discarded ex, Joan, went off to a convent and later was sainted – talk about turning a raw deal into a heavenly one!) Many a lesser noble simply lived apart from their spouse for decades, conducting love affairs on the side and praying for a papal annulment or a timely widowhood. A few took more *extreme* measures – a dash of poison here, a staged riding accident there – when patience (and piety) wore thin.

All this conniving makes modern divorces look as simple as a trip to city hall. Sure, today's breakups can be messy, but at least you don't need to prove you're third cousins or get a committee of nuns to approve your split. Our forebears had to twist both logic and law into pretzels to escape unhappy marriages. The next time someone says, "They don't make love like they used to," remember they don't un-make it like they used to either – thank goodness.

- **Marriage Lesson:** Where there's a will (and no divorce), there's a loophole. If you can't split up the normal way, get creative – whether that means finding a long-lost cousin or dusting off a nun's habit.

- **Takeaway:** The next time someone complains their divorce was dramatic, remind them that at least it didn't require papal approval, a public bedding trial, or sending their ex to live out life in a cloister. *Perspective* is everything.

5. Modern Crown Cracks – Even fairy-tale marriages fail: Britain's Charles and Diana's very public split in 1996 showed that not even royalty are guaranteed a happily ever after (no guillotine needed)

By now we've seen how historic royals handled bad marriages with everything from swords to shenanigans. But what about our modern tiara-wearing lovebirds? For a glimpse at a contemporary royal breakup – mercifully sans executions and exile – we turn to one of the 20th century's most famous failed fairy tales: Prince Charles and Princess Diana. If Henry VIII's divorces shook the church, Charles and Diana's split shook the tabloids (and gave the British monarchy one of its biggest headaches since, well, the American Revolution).

It all started so promisingly. In 1981, Charles, Prince of Wales – heir to the British throne – married Lady Diana Spencer in a storybook wedding so glittery and grand that *Cinderella* herself would've swooned. It was broadcast to hundreds of millions around the globe; Diana arrived at St. Paul's Cathedral in a glass coach, decked in ivory silk with a 25-foot train, marrying her Prince Charming. The union of the dashing prince and the shy 20-year-old nursery school teacher was billed as a real-life fairy tale. Spoiler alert: the fairy tale hit the rocks pretty fast.

Behind palace doors, the marriage struggled. Charles was 12 years older and set in his ways; Diana was young, charismatic, and soon more popular than any royal had a right to be. They had two sons (Princes William and Harry) but little marital bliss. Charles never fully let go of his longtime love (and former girlfriend) Camilla Parker Bowles, and Diana felt isolated and betrayed as that shadow loomed over their marriage. By the late 1980s, both were straying: Diana found companionship elsewhere, and Charles rekindled his romance with Camilla.

The difference from the old days? No chopping block or convenient convent, but instead a feeding frenzy in the media. The royals' troubles exploded into public view in the early 1990s, with scandal after scandal. In 1992 – the Queen's self-proclaimed "annus horribilis" (horrible year) – Charles and Diana separated, and the news was everywhere. Diana poured her heart out in a tell-all biography and later an explosive TV interview. Charles's private, intimate phone chat with Camilla leaked (and made everyone listening turn bright red). The world learned that this fairy-tale marriage had more drama than a season of *Dallas*. Diana memorably quipped, "There were three of us in this marriage, so it was a bit crowded," throwing the classiest shade ever at Charles and Camilla. The tabloids ate it up, splashing the dirty details across front pages daily.

By 1996, even the Queen had seen enough – she urged the couple to divorce and put an end to the spectacle. The official split came in August 1996, after 15 years of a very public union. Diana walked away with a sizable settlement and retained her title "Princess of Wales," but she was stripped of the honorific "Her Royal Highness" (the palace's subtle way of saying she was out of the royal inner circle). Charles was free to eventually marry Camilla (which he did in 2005, with far less pomp – and zero televised opulence).

No, this breakup didn't spawn a new church or send anyone to the scaffold, but it marked a turning point for the modern monarchy. It proved that even with velvet robes and diamond tiaras, a marriage can crumble like any other. The image of the perfect prince and princess was revealed to be just that: an image. In the aftermath, the royal family had to modernize (a tad) and accept that divorce, while messy, wasn't a mortal sin or the end of the Crown. In fact, in the very generation before, Charles's own great-uncle King Edward VIII had to give up his throne in 1936 to marry a divorced woman. By the 1990s, a Prince of Wales could get divorced and still eventually become King – my, how times change.

The saga of Charles and Diana had no fairy-tale ending – Diana's tragic death in a car crash in 1997 sealed that for good. But it did leave a legacy. It showed that royalty aren't exempt from the trials of love and loss. It brought a new openness (and caution) to how royal marriages are treated in the public eye. And it reassured us of one thing: at least nowadays when a royal marriage fails, the only thing that might roll is someone's reputation – not their head.

- **Marriage Lesson:** Even fairy-tale weddings can turn into pumpkin soup. Being royal doesn't guarantee romance will last – it just guarantees your breakup will be a public spectacle.

- **Takeaway:** Modern royals prove that "happily ever after" isn't guaranteed. The big difference today? If it all falls apart, you might lose your HRH title, but you *won't* lose your head – and that's progress by any standard of royal history.

Chapter 7

Un-tying the Knot, DIY-Style – Bizarre Divorce Customs of Common Folk

So, you think your divorce was messy? Trust us, it's probably a snooze-fest compared to the wild DIY divorce customs from history we're about to unpack. Buckle up (or untie that knot, as it were), because this chapter is taking you on a time-traveling tour of marital breakups that make Las Vegas divorces look downright pedestrian. We're talking about everyday folks—no kings or queens here—who found hilariously creative ways to say "I don't" after saying "I do."

In this irreverent romp through the ages, you'll meet a Cherokee wife who didn't need a lawyer to kick her hubby to the curb (literally), an Englishman who tried to hawk his spouse like a used car (rope and all), and a few other colorful characters who prove that breaking up has always been hard (or bizarre) to do. By the end, you might just pick up a few cheeky marriage lessons—because if history has taught us anything, it's that the road to divorce is paved with good intentions, terrible ideas, and the occasional public auction. Let's dive in!

Packing His Bags – In old Cherokee and Hopi tradition, a wife could end the marriage by simply leaving her husband's belongings outside the home

Ever fantasized about ending an argument by literally throwing your partner's stuff out the front door? In certain old Cherokee and Hopi traditions, that wasn't just a fantasy—it was basically the official divorce procedure. Forget legal papers or couples therapy; if wifey dearest was done with your nonsense, she'd pack up your clothes, hunting gear, favorite moccasins, maybe even that beloved tomahawk, and unceremoniously dump it all outside the dwelling. Congratulations, dear husband: you've been served, indigenous style.

This was the ultimate "hefty bag" hint. Picture the scene: You come home from a long day of whatever 18th-century Cherokee husbands did (perhaps a hunting trip or a really intense stickball game), and there's your saddle, your spare loincloth, and that ugly spear-thrower your mother gave you—all piled up outside like yesterday's trash. In modern terms, it's the equivalent of finding all your stuff in a box to the left, to the left (yes, Beyoncé would approve). The message was crystal clear: You've worn out your welcome, pal. No need to fight about who gets the dog or the teepee; the wife kept the house, and you kept… the horse and the now slightly-used loincloth, presumably.

What's really intriguing (and frankly progressive) is that in these communities, women held the power to initiate the split. The Cherokee and Hopi were matrilineal societies, meaning the home and kids typically stayed with the wife's clan. So if she booted you out, you were literally going back to your mother's house. Talk about a reverse Uno card in the game of marriage. One minute you're the man of the house; the next, you're hoisting your belongings on your back, doing the walk of shame back to mom's place under the amused eyes of the whole village. At least you didn't need to pay alimony—just maybe apologize to your mom for coming back so soon.

In today's world, tossing your partner's stuff on the lawn usually precedes a call to a divorce lawyer (or the cops, if things get ugly). But Cherokee and Hopi wives handled it in-house—literally outside the house. Sure, it lacks the drama of a courtroom showdown, but there's a certain satisfying simplicity to it. It's like the universe's fastest eviction notice: Husband, meet curb. Curb, meet husband. The community likely knew what it meant too. No reality TV cameras needed; neighbors would see the impromptu yard sale of hubby's personal effects and think, "Welp, looks like the poor guy is single again. Wonder what he did this time…"

Modern analogies practically write themselves. Imagine a suburban scenario: wife changes the locks and piles hubby's Xbox, golf clubs, and beer-stained recliner on the driveway. Add a sign that says "Free to a *new* home" and post it on Instagram for maximum effect. In a way, the Cherokee and Hopi method was the original "clean break." No lawyers, no messy paperwork—just one not-so-subtle gesture that spoke louder than a thousand divorce decrees: *Pack your bags, bucko, this marriage is toast.*

Marriage Lesson: When everything you own is suddenly in a box outside, your marriage might need more than a weekend couples' retreat—sometimes it's just over, and that's your cue to literally hit the road.

Market Value – 18th-century English husbands literally sold their wives at the market with a rope around the wife's neck, auctioneer-style, as a makeshift divorce

From the "you can't be serious" files of history: there was a time in 18th and even 19th-century England when a man could *literally* lead his wife to the market with a rope around her neck and auction her off to the highest bidder. Yes, you read that correctly. No, this isn't the fever dream of a Monty Python sketch; it actually happened. Think of it as eBay for unhappy marriages, except the "Buy It Now" option involved a live auctioneer and a crowd of villagers munching on meat pies.

Why on earth would this happen? Well, formal divorces in ye olde England were about as affordable as a private island. So ordinary blokes, upon realizing that 'till death do us part' was too long to wait, got creative. They figured, hey, if you can't join 'em (in holy matrimony), beat 'em – or rather, sell 'em. It was the working man's DIY divorce. The disgruntled husband would put a halter or ribbon on his wife – part humiliation, part literal leash – and parade her around the local market or tavern like a prize heifer up for auction. He'd holler something like, "Step right up, gents, have I got a deal for you today! One wife, slightly used, cooks a mean stew, doesn't snore (much). What am I bid?"

Crowds would gather because, let's face it, humans have always loved a good spectacle (and maybe some were genuinely in the market for a pre-owned wife – these were lonely times). The wife, at least in theory, had to agree to all this – and often the "buyer" was conveniently her new lover, making the whole transaction more of a formality (albeit a cringey one). Essentially, Husband #1 hands off wifey to Suitor #2, who pays a token price, and voilá: old marriage effectively canceled, new marriage unofficially on. It's like trading in your Ford for a Chevy, except Ford = your spouse, and the trade-in process involves public heckling.

Some of these sales were absurdly casual. One famous case in 1852 (yes, this insanity lingered into the 19th century) saw a fellow in Nottingham bring his wife to the town square with a nice new rope around her neck. He announced, "Here's my wife for sale, starting bid two shillings and sixpence – rope included, folks, it's worth sixpence alone!" I'm not making that up; he literally touted the rope's value like a true salesman. In the end, Wife was sold for the bargain price of one shilling to a chap named Burrows. The trio – seller, buyer, and the presumably relieved wife – then allegedly went to the pub to sign a document formalizing the swap, probably over a round of ales. Nothing seals a bizarre divorce deal like a pint, right?

It wasn't *technically* legal, but it was socially accepted enough that authorities mostly turned a blind eye (imagine the paperwork if they didn't). For the husbands, it beat waiting around for Parliament to grant a divorce. For the wives, well, hopefully they got a better deal with Husband 2. One can only hope the new guy at least paid more than the price of a sheep. Speaking of which, the whole affair really did resemble a livestock sale – sometimes the auction took place right by the cattle pens. Wives were being sold among sheep and cows, which is about as metaphorically on-point as it gets for how those societies viewed women's rights. (Note: very *baaaadly*.)

Modern comparison? Picture a disgruntled dude posting on Craigslist: "Wife for sale – $50 OBO, no scammers, serious inquiries only." The ad would get flagged in five seconds today (and the dude would get a swift visit from both the police and maybe a psychiatrist). But in Georgian England, it was the talk of the town, a sorta-not-quite-legit divorce that everyone understood. The closest we get now are those reality TV shows where exes swap partners, but even those have more paperwork and fewer sheep.

At least one novelist, Thomas Hardy, was so appalled that he opened his novel *The Mayor of Casterbridge* with a drunken husband selling his wife – and readers of the time were like, "Yep, that's a thing that happens." Outlandish, yes, but true.

Marriage Lesson: If your spouse ever suggests a "trip to the market" and starts looking for rope, you might want to lawyer up – or run. In any era, know your worth (and it's definitely more than one shilling).

"I Divorce Thee" x3 – The now-banned triple talaq allowed a Muslim man to instantly divorce his wife by saying "talaq" (I divorce you) three times – even via text

Ever wish you could end an argument by just *saying* the last word – literally? Well, in the case of the (now thankfully banned) practice of triple talaq, the "last word" was actually the last three words, and they ended more than just the argument. In certain communities, a Muslim man could instantly end his marriage by saying "talaq" – meaning "I divorce you" – three times in a row. That's it. Three magic words and *poof*, the marriage disappears in a cloud of djinn smoke. It was like a verbal control-alt-delete for your wedding vows.

If saying it out loud wasn't convenient (perhaps the missus wasn't in earshot for your dramatic pronouncement?), no worries – modern technology had you covered. Some enterprising fellows delivered the triple whammy via phone call, WhatsApp, even text message. Yes, the dreaded "we need to talk" text had an even more diabolical cousin: the "talaq talaq talaq" triple text. Imagine glancing at your phone and seeing a message from your husband that's essentially: "I divorce you. I divorce you. I divorce you." At first, you'd think he sat on his phone and pocket-texted the same thing thrice. But nope – he meant it, and congrats, you're suddenly his ex. No court, no discussion, not even an emoji to soften the blow.

To put it in perspective, this is basically the *polar opposite* of how most divorces work. Regular people have to file papers, wait months, argue over who gets the cat. But with triple talaq, one party (the husband) just drops the mic – or the phone – and walks away. It makes Vegas quickie divorces look like long, drawn-out Russian novels. At least in Vegas you have to sign something; here you just needed a working larynx or cell signal. Talk about a one-sided conversation! The wife's opinion in the matter carried as much weight as a cat's opinion of algebra.

The ease of it was ripe for satire. It's the kind of thing where you'd expect a genie to pop out and warn, "Be careful what you wish for, buddy." Say "Beetlejuice" three times and you summon a mischievous ghost; say "talaq" three times and you summon a divorce lawyer – actually, scratch that, no lawyer needed, that's the whole point. One could imagine a hapless husband, mid-fight over leaving the toilet seat up, blurting out "talaq, talaq, talaq!" like a frustrated magic spell. Cue a puff of smoke, and *ding!* you are now unsubscribed from Marriage Newsletter. The fine print? You can't re-subscribe unless your ex-wife marries someone else and that marriage ends (seriously, Google "nikah halala" for that saga). Sounds like a bad plot from a telenovela, but it was reality for some.

This practice has been largely kicked to the curb in the modern world – many countries (including India in 2017) outlawed it, presumably after collectively saying, "Dude, not cool." One too many guys apparently took the easy way out, leaving bewildered ex-wives in their wake. It was as if half the population had a cheat code for marriage ("Up, up, down, down, talaq, talaq, talaq, start – Marriage Over!"), and finally the system said game over to the cheat.

On the bright side (if there was one), at least it was concise. No long speeches, no "It's not you, it's me" (the ultimate irony: it *was* always you, not her). Just a trio of words and a marital vanishing act. Think of the legendary British comedy catchphrase: "And now for something completely different – my marital status." Only it wasn't comedy for the poor women who got hit with the verbal tripwire.

Modern equivalent? Maybe a celebrity tweeting "#Divorced" three times and calling it a day. (If only it were that easy, right Kanye?) Actually, we did have a modern celeb moment: Russell Brand reportedly ended his marriage with Katy Perry via text (just once, not thrice – but it only took one message to do the job). Not exactly triple talaq, but the same energy of bad form. Pro tip: if you must end a marriage, maybe do it face-to-face, or at least with a phone call and some basic decency.

Marriage Lesson: Words have power – choose them (and the number of times you repeat them) wisely. And if your partner starts repeating phrases at you like a broken record, maybe check if they're trying to abracadabra themselves into being single.

Ring Return Refund – Folklore in Merry Old England held that if a husband neglected his wife, she could dump him by handing back his ring, no court needed

Now, for a bit of folklore from Merry Old England – a place and time when apparently you didn't always need King Henry VIII-level clout to ditch your spouse. Legend has it that if a husband was chronically neglectful (think: spends all day at ye olde tavern, forgets anniversaries, hasn't bathed since Michaelmas), his long-suffering wife had a simple, elegant exit strategy: hand the chap his ring back and pronounce the marriage done. No judge, no church tribunal, just plop – ring in hand, marriage over. Consider it the medieval equivalent of, "Here, take your ring and don't let the door hit you on the way out."

It's a bit like returning a faulty product to the store. "Sorry, this husband is not as advertised – I'd like a full refund." The ring was basically the receipt. By giving it back, wifey was saying, "Your services as a partner are no longer required; kindly see yourself out." One imagines the husband blinking in astonishment, perhaps sputtering, "B-but you can't just—" and the wife casually responding, "Oh, I most certainly can. Cheers, darling!" (If she had a mic, it'd be dropped right here.)

Of course, this was folklore, not exactly law, so results may have varied. But the mere idea that a wife could self-serve her own divorce like that must have been both empowering and terrifying (at least for husbands who spent too many late nights at Ye Olde Pub). It flips the script on that classic marriage vow. Forget "till death do us part" – more like "till neglect do I part, and at that point I'm handing back your stupid ring." Perhaps this little legend was a subtle reminder to husbands: don't take your wife for granted, or you might find a shiny band shoved back in your face and your dinner no longer on the table.

In a way, this is the romanticized, fairy-tale version of divorce. No messy legal battle, no dividing the estate – just a symbolic gesture and *poof,* each goes their separate way. If only it were that easy! If this custom had actually caught on widely, divorce lawyers today would be about as useful as a chocolate teapot. Alas (or thankfully), reality is more complicated. But it's a fun thought: imagine if every time a spouse felt ignored or underappreciated they could just mail back the wedding ring with a "Thanks, but no thanks" note. The postal service would need a dedicated "Return to Sender: Ex-Husband" department.

Modern culture still echoes a bit of this concept when a scorned bride or groom dramatically throws the ring at their partner during a fight. (We've all seen that movie scene.) In our folklore scenario, that dramatic toss wasn't just anger – it was legally binding enough in the court of public opinion. Talk about killing two birds with one ring: express your fury *and* finalize your breakup in one go.

So gentlemen of yore, if your wife ever offered you your ring back with a sweet-yet-sinister smile, that was your cue that you'd epically bungled things. She was reclaiming her freedom, one precious metal band at a time. And ladies, it was a reminder that even in patriarchal times, a neglected wife could deploy the ultimate "I'm done with this" gesture and walk away without so much as a backward glance or a law court in sight.

Marriage Lesson: A ring is a symbol of love and commitment – but if you don't honor that commitment, don't be surprised if it comes flying back at you. Consider it the world's smallest (and priciest) frisbee of marital doom.

When in Rome, Just Walk Away – In Ancient Rome, divorces were easy: spouses could dissolve the marriage by mutual consent (no lawyers, just ciao!), leading many Romans to have multiple exes by age 20

Finally, we arrive in Ancient Rome – the land of togas, triumphs, and... surprisingly chill divorces. If you thought modern no-fault divorce was progressive, the Romans were way ahead of the curve. Basically, if a marriage wasn't working out, a Roman husband *or wife* could say "*vale*" (Latin for "bye-bye, darling") and that was that. Both spouses just agreed to call it quits, divided the household knick-knacks, and moved on with their lives. No tribunals, no dramatic legal battles – not even a need to specify a reason. The law eventually boiled down to "eh, if you consider yourself not married anymore, you're not." Talk about simple! They didn't even have to sign anything until centuries later. Official divorce papers weren't required until around 449 AD, meaning for most of Roman history, breaking up was literally as easy as *breaking up.*

This meant serial marriages were practically a hobby for some Romans. Elite socialites swapped spouses faster than a game of musical chairs (with Jupiter's blessing, presumably). By the time some Roman patricians hit the big *two-oh*, they had enough exes to form a support group. Wedding #1 at 16, divorce by 17, remarried by 18, onto Ex #3 by 20 – it sounds like a reality show, *Real Housewives of the Roman Republic.* (Except the "housewives" could be husbands too, and nobody was particularly scandalized by it.) One poet joked about a woman who had eight husbands in five years – and that was in an era without Tinder. Even emperors got in on the action: some married women who'd been divorced multiple times, and nobody batted an eye. Emperor Augustus – a bit of a moralist – tried to encourage stable marriages with laws and penalties, but even in his own family, people were trading partners like charioteers swapping horses.

Imagine a society where you could accrue ex-spouses before you could legally rent a car (by today's standards). That was Rome. It was almost *too* easy. You think Hollywood stars have quickie marriages? In Rome, you could have a whole string of "starter marriages" before your first wrinkle. If Ross from *Friends* had been Roman, his three divorces would've barely qualified as a slow week.

The Romans even had a saying – "*matrimonia debent esse libera*" – marriages ought to be free (as in free to leave). They understood that forcing unhappy people to stay hitched was a recipe for drama (and Romans loved drama, but only the on-stage kind). So they set up a system where if you both agreed things weren't working out, you'd simply part ways amicably… or as amicably as any split can be. Property was usually kept separate during marriage, so dividing stuff was straightforward. The kids usually stayed with the father by default, but given Dad might remarry in a month and Mom the month after, the Roman family tree often looked more like a wreath.

Now, it wasn't *all* sunshine and rose petals – emotions still ran high, and not every divorce was mutual. Technically, one spouse could dump the other unilaterally (yes, even by surprise). Imagine coming home to find your partner gone and a message that basically says "By the way, we're not married anymore. Ciao!" Awkward. But generally, it was a society where divorce carried little stigma. You wouldn't lose all your friends just because you changed spouses like outfits. In fact, staying in a miserable marriage when you could easily leave would probably get you more weird looks.

When we compare this to, say, Henry VIII (you know, that English king who collected ex-wives and occasionally their heads), one can't help but shake one's head. If old Henry had been a Roman, he could've saved himself a whole lot of trouble. No need to start a new church or execute spouses – he could've filed for divorce Roman-style (Step 1: Announce "I'm out," Step 2: There is no Step 2) and gone on his merry way, wife #2 on arm, no bloodshed required.

So yeah, when in Rome, you really could "just walk away" from a marriage. It was divorce without the drama – or at least without the legal bureaucracy. Of course, human nature being what it is, I'm sure there was still plenty of drama (jealous exes, quick rebounds, gossip at the Forum – "Did you hear Decimus left Tullia and took up with that new harpist girl?"). But legally speaking, it was no muss, no fuss. Many Romans likely had more former in-laws than you have Facebook friends.

Marriage Lesson: Marriage might be easy to enter and exit, but collecting exes like souvenirs can be its own circus. Commitment shouldn't be taken lightly – even if the law says you can swap spouses faster than a gladiator changes swords, maybe think twice (or thrice) before saying "I do" (and "I don't" and "I do again").

Chapter 8

Lawfully Wedded Weird – Outrageous Marriage Laws and Loopholes

Perfect. I'll write Chapter 8 as a flowing, cheeky narrative with the five section titles as anchors. Expect absurd legal loopholes, toothless brides, and blackbird body counts—with modern pop culture and marital insights woven throughout. I'll let you know once it's ready.

Lawfully Wedded Weird – Outrageous Marriage Laws and Loopholes

Marriage is a beautiful commitment – or so they say. But as we're about to discover, around the world (and right here at home) there have been some truly bizarre ways to say "I do" and some ridiculous rules to follow after you've tied the knot. In this chapter, we take a lighthearted look at five outrageous marriage laws and loopholes that will make you question everything you thought you knew about wedded bliss. From marrying a ghost (yes, really) to weddings where *nobody* shows up, from monster-in-law mayhem to colonial-era bird hunting bachelors and toothless wives in Vermont – it's clear that love not only laughs at locksmiths, it also has a good chuckle at legislators.

Ready for a wild ride down the aisle of absurdity? Cue the wedding march (playfully, on kazoos perhaps), and let's dive into these true tales of matrimonial madness. *(Don't worry, you won't need a lawyer for this ceremony – just a sense of humor.)*

Marrying the Dead – French necrogamy law (dating to WWI) lets you marry your deceased sweetheart under strict conditions

"Till death do us part" is a lovely sentiment – unless you're French, apparently, in which case *death* might just be a minor bureaucratic hurdle. Welcome to necrogamy, the charming practice of marrying someone who is, shall we say, not among the living. In France, it's not a Halloween prank or a Tim Burton movie plot – it's actually legal (under very strict conditions, mind you) to wed your dearly departed sweetheart. Talk about undying love!

This unusual law dates back to World War I, when heartbroken fiancées of fallen soldiers reportedly asked to marry their dead sweethearts by proxy to honor their memory. Rather than telling these grieving lovers "C'est la vie" and moving on, the French authorities eventually said "oui" – with lots of red tape attached, naturellement. Fast forward to 1959: a tragedy involving a dam burst left a young woman bereaved and still longing to be married to her late fiancé. Her plea reached all the way to the President of France, who must have been feeling particularly romantic (or sympathetic). In response, France officially clarified the law, allowing posthumous marriages under specific circumstances. Leave it to the French to make even ghostly romance sound poetic and *bureaucratic* at the same time.

So, how does one marry a corpse without causing an episode of *The Walking Dead: Wedding Edition*? First, you can't just wander into Père Lachaise cemetery, find a handsome ghost, and say "Je t'aime, let's get hitched." Non, non, non. You must prove that the *deceased* intended to marry you while they were still alive. In other words, there had to be a wedding on the horizon (rings purchased, dates set, perhaps an Etsy order of 200 monogrammed napkins) before your partner shuffled off this mortal coil. You then petition the President of the Republic for permission to hold the wedding. Yes, the French President basically plays Cupid-from-beyond-the-grave in these cases. We can only imagine the paperwork – a marriage license and a death certificate get combined in ways no bridezilla ever envisioned.

If approval is granted (also needs the Justice Minister's sign-off, because why not involve the whole government in your love life?), a strange ceremony takes place. The living bride or groom stands next to a photo of their late partner – wedding attire optional but encouraged for full dramatic effect – and the vows are adjusted for the... situation. They tactfully omit "till death do us part," for obvious reasons, and instead of saying "I do," the living spouse says "I did." That's not a punchline; that's literally what they say in the French ceremony. It's both touching and darkly comic – as if the officiant is declaring, "This marriage is retroactively effective yesterday, and death be darned." The first time I heard that, I nearly did a spit-take with my Bordeaux. "I did" – past tense – because one of you is *past tense*. Gotta admire the French for their commitment to verb conjugation accuracy even in matrimony.

Now, you might wonder: why would anyone go through with this? Well, aside from the emotional closure, a posthumous marriage does not grant all the normal perks – sorry, no inheritance or tax benefits, mes amis. It's truly a labor of love (and paperwork). It's also quite rare. Only a few cases per year make it through. One notable story was a woman named Magali who married her dead fiancé in 2009; he had died in a car accident just days before their wedding date. She stood beside his photograph at the town hall and pledged her eternal love, proving that not even a head-on collision could derail her happily ever after. It's heartbreaking, yes, but also oddly heartwarming that the law allowed her that closure. In a way, French necrogamy is the ultimate expression of *la grande romance* – or maybe just the ultimate example of French exceptionalism. ("We'll even out-love death. Top that, America!")

For the rest of us, this law raises plenty of eyebrows (and a few questions). Do you send thank-you notes after a posthumous wedding? Does the caterer charge a ghost guest fee? And who cuts the cake? (I'm guessing the bride slices it in front of the framed photo and politely eats both pieces – one for her and one for the late groom, who's watching from the great beyond with a thumbs up.) The whole thing sounds like a dark comedy scene. Hollywood, are you listening? We've got the script for *Weekend at Bernie's Wedding* ready to go.

All joking aside, it's a testament to how absurdly far bureaucracy will bend for love – at least in France. It gives a whole new meaning to the phrase "love never dies." In France, love can literally *get a marriage license and a day in court to prove it.* If that isn't commitment, I don't know what is.

Marriage Lesson: "Till death do us part" is just a suggestion – at least in France. True love can transcend the grave… provided you fill out the proper forms and get presidential approval (because even eternal love needs a rubber stamp).

Proxy Knot-Tying – In Montana you can have a double proxy wedding: neither the bride nor groom shows up, and stand-ins get you legally hitched from afar

If the French can marry ghosts, surely Americans can top that? Welcome to Montana, where we do one better: you can marry a *live person* without either of you attending the wedding! That's right – in Big Sky Country, you might say "I do" by telephone, email, or perhaps telepathy, while two complete strangers stand in for you and your beloved at the altar. This is the magical world of the double proxy wedding, the ultimate solution for couples who love commitment but hate ceremonies (or are just inconveniently located halfway around the globe).

Picture this scene: A charming little courthouse in Montana, a couple of well-dressed locals exchanging vows before a clerk, kissing for the cameras... and then immediately mailing the marriage certificate to the *actual* bride and groom who are thousands of miles away, possibly Skyping in to witness their own nuptials with popcorn in hand. It sounds like a rom-com starring Sandra Bullock and Ryan Reynolds, but nope – it's totally legal, at least in Montana. In every other state, at least one half of the couple must be physically present to say "I do." But Montana says, "Why stop at one? Heck, neither of you needs to show up. Go ranch some cattle or climb a mountain; we got this."

How did this absentee matrimony come to be? The roots of Montana's proxy wedding law stretch back to the 1860s, when Montana was a rugged territory full of miners, cowboys, and not nearly enough young ladies. Those lonely bachelors out in the gold fields still fell in love (or arranged to, via letters) with sweethearts back

East. But traveling home for a wedding was dangerous, expensive, and time-consuming (no direct flights to Montana in the 19th century, imagine that!). So territorial law allowed a proxy to stand in for the absent groom so he could marry his faraway fiancée without leaving the mine. Fast forward a century or so, add the progressive idea of gender equality (hey, women can be absent brides too!), and Montana eventually said, "Heck, who needs either party present? We trust ya. We'll marry you in absentia, double proxy, no problem." By state law, as long as one of the couple is either a Montana resident or on active military duty, you can hire two stand-ins to exchange your vows for you. It's basically the InstaWedding service – you could literally be sitting on a beach in Bali and get married in Montana simultaneously. (So much for destination weddings – Montana turned *not going* into the biggest destination of all!)

Modern technology has, unsurprisingly, made this even more popular. During the COVID-19 pandemic, when travel was nearly impossible and even being in the same room carried the risk of adding "'til illness do us part" to the vows, double proxy marriages skyrocketed. One Montana county reported going from a few hundred proxy marriages a year to over four thousand! Who knew that the ultimate wedding hack was hiding in the Treasure State all along? Meanwhile, overworked county clerks in Montana became inadvertent wedding planners for the world – churning out marriage licenses like a Las Vegas chapel on overtime. (Except in Vegas at least the couple has to stumble in at 3 AM; in Montana you can stay in your PJs and let someone else do the stumbling for you.)

There's even a husband-and-wife entrepreneurial duo in Flathead County, Montana, who have made a thriving business out of these peculiar nuptials. For a few hundred bucks, Tom and Teresa (local proxies extraordinaire) will gladly be you and your spouse-for-a-day. They'll recite the vows, sign the papers, even share a celebratory kiss on *your* behalf (strictly optional, but c'mon, they're professionals). They perform hundreds of ceremonies a year without ever meeting the actual bride or groom – talk about strangers tying your knot! At this point, Tom and Teresa have probably been married *to each other* hundreds of times in proxy world, all while their real marriage stays intact. It's like *50 First Dates*; except it's *500 Proxy Weddings* and they collect a fee each time. Honestly, respect: they found a way to attend a ton of weddings and never have to buy a single gift.

From a certain angle, a double proxy wedding is basically the ultimate introvert marriage. Hate public speaking? No problem, someone else will say your vows. Can't stand dressing up? Stay in your sweatpants, they'll don the gown and tux. Dread your weird Uncle Bob causing a scene at the reception? There *is* no reception – you're already on your honeymoon or deployed overseas or whatever, and Uncle Bob wasn't invited because, well, no one was. It's marriage by delegation, the UPS of love: absolutely, positively, *get hitched overnight.*

Of course, there are critics. Some say it takes the *meaning* out of marriage. But hey, if both parties consent and the state's cool with it, who are we to judge? Think of the possibilities: celebrity couples dodging paparazzi could secretly wed via proxy (so far, surprisingly, none of the Kardashians have tried this – maybe they actually *like* the media circus?). And consider how convenient this is for long-distance lovers and military members deployed abroad: they can secure the legal benefits of marriage (health insurance, anyone?) without one of them AWOL-ing from duty or flying halfway across the world. It's love *and* practicality rolled into one weird little package.

The mental image still makes me giggle, though. I imagine a beautiful Montana meadow with nobody there except two hired stand-ins reading heartfelt vows off a script like it's the *Academy Awards* ("I'm just honored to accept this marriage on behalf of John and Jane, who unfortunately couldn't be here today..."). Perhaps a webcam on a tripod Skypes the real couple so they can at least cheer from afar. And when the officiant says "You may now kiss... whoever's standing next to you," the proxies dutifully peck each other on the cheek. I hope they at least send the couple a selfie to commemorate the big day.

In the end, Montana's double proxy marriage law proves that where there's a will (and a weird law), there's a way. Love finds a way – even if that way involves FedExing your marriage license from 5,000 miles away. Is it romantic? Debatable. Is it efficient? Absolutely. And very, very quirky.

Marriage Lesson: If you truly love someone, set them free – or better yet, let someone else stand in for you at the altar. Who says you actually have to *show up* for your own wedding? True love is flexible, and in Montana, it can be downright absentee.

Mother-in-Law Insurance – Wichita, Kansas once required husbands to be nice to their mothers-in-law or it was legal grounds for divorce

Ah, mothers-in-law – the classic punchline of so many marriage jokes. But in one corner of Kansas, the *in-law* went from punchline to legal headline. Believe it or not, Wichita, Kansas apparently once had a law on the books that basically said: *"Be nice to your mother-in-law, or you're gonna be single."* In other words, if a husband mistreated his wife's mother, it could be used as grounds for the wife to divorce his uncouth behind. Talk about backing up the *"Happy wife, happy life"* mantra with some legal muscle – more like "Happy mother-in-law, or no wife!"

Now, I can hear some of you cheering, "Yes! Protect the moms!" while others are gasping, "Good grief, what about protecting the poor husbands from *their* in-laws?!" Let's set the scene: Imagine a 1950s Wichita housewife, June Cleaver style, except June is fuming because Ward was rude to her mother during Sunday dinner. (Maybe he dared suggest Mom's casserole was a tad overcooked – the nerve!). Under this bizarre law, June could march down to the courthouse on Monday and file for divorce, citing "he dissed my mama" as a legitimate legal grievance. And the local judge, instead of laughing her out of the building, might actually say, "You know, the lady's got a point – law's the law, Ward. You should've eaten that casserole with a smile. Divorce granted!"

It sounds like a sitcom plot – *Everybody Loves Raymond*, Kansas Edition, where Debra can legally dump Ray the minute he sasses Marie. In fact, if that law were alive today, half the husbands in America would be nervously taking their mothers-in-law out for spa days and shopping sprees, just to build up goodwill (and divorce immunity). Wichita husbands back then must have been on their best behavior, at least when the wife's family was in town. You can picture a fellow reminding himself: *Smile, compliment her hat, pretend you adore her fruitcake... your marriage depends on it, man!* It's like marital insurance: pay the premium of politeness, or the policy (your marriage) gets canceled.

How did such a law come to exist? One theory: perhaps Kansas, being a historically conservative place, had very limited grounds for divorce back in the day. (Many states only allowed fault-based divorce for things like abuse, abandonment, adultery, etc.) Maybe some clever Kansas lawmaker – likely with a meddling mother-in-law of his own – thought, "You know what counts as cruelty? Insulting the mother-in-law! That should be a marital crime!" Alternatively, maybe *so many* wives were attempting to rid themselves of loutish husbands by saying "He's mean to my mom" that Wichita decided to explicitly make it either valid or invalid in statute. It's truly a toss-up whether the law was pro-mother-in-law ("be nice or else") or pro-husband ("sorry, ladies, disliking your mom isn't a reason to leave him"). The legend, however, most commonly tells it as pro-mom: husband must be nice or face the legal consequences.

Regardless of the legislative intent, the mere fact this was written down in an ordinance or law is comedy gold. It elevates the stereotypical familial squabble to the level of jurisprudence. Did they have to establish a threshold for "mistreatment," one wonders? Like, is forgetting your mother-in-law's birthday a mild misdemeanor, but telling a "mother-in-law joke" in her presence a felony offense? If you rolled your eyes behind her back when she offered unsolicited parenting advice, would the Wichita police marriage unit come knocking? One imagines a hapless husband standing before a judge: "Sir, on the date of May 5th, did you or did you not refer to your wife's mother as – I quote – 'an overbearing old hen'?" And the guy, sweating bullets: "Um, I may have *implied* something to that effect—" and BAM, the gavel hits, "Divorce granted! And son, you'd best send flowers on Mother's Day *for life* if you ever plan to remarry in this town!"

For wives, this law was like having a nuclear option in the nightstand drawer. Sure, you *could* use it, but the fall-out's huge – nobody wants to actually blow up a marriage over mom (we hope). Still, it must have given some leverage: "Honey, I know you don't want to take Mom to that bingo tournament, but *remember the law.*" (Cue husband, gritting teeth: "Yes, dear, I'll go warm up the car.") In that sense, maybe it *prevented* a few fights or encouraged at least a facade of civility. Or conversely, maybe some devilish wives used it as a threat unfairly. We'll never know the countless domestic Cold Wars waged with this peculiar statute in the background.

Modern sensibilities find this all rather antiquated and humorous. Today, if your husband is being a jerk to your mom, you don't need a special law – you have Dr. Phil, therapy, or in worst case, the generic "irreconcilable differences" catch-all. But kudos to Wichita for once acknowledging the very real family dynamic: when you marry someone, you often marry their family too (for better or worse!). And sometimes, *worse* wears a floral-print dress and asks pointed questions about your life choices over Thanksgiving dinner.

While it's unclear when this law was scrapped (I'd bet it's not enforced now – sorry, monster-in-laws, you missed your chance), it lives on in the pantheon of weird marriage laws. It also lives on in every comedian's repertoire of marriage one-liners. But unlike the jokes, for Wichita couples it was deadly serious once upon a time.

So, next time your spouse's mom criticizes your cooking or redecorates your living room without asking, take a deep breath. It could be worse – you could be legally required to grin and bear it under threat of divorce. And if you *are* in Kansas, maybe check the local ordinances, just to be safe. (Or better yet, just be nice – it's easier in the long run, trust me.)

Marriage Lesson: You don't just marry a person; you marry their family. So play nice with the in-laws – in some places it wasn't just good manners, it was the law! A happy mother-in-law can mean a happy marriage… and a less risky one, at least in Wichita.

Fowl Play – A 1770s law in Truro, Massachusetts demanded bachelors kill six blackbirds or three crows each before they were allowed to marry

As if finding a soulmate isn't hard enough, imagine you also had to present a pile of dead birds to city hall before getting a marriage license. Yes, that sounds utterly loony, but in colonial Massachusetts the struggle was real. In the quaint Cape Cod town of Truro (back in the 1770s), bachelors had to literally prove their worth by hunting birds – six blackbirds or three crows, to be exact – *before* they could take a wife. Talk about a bizarre dowry system: "I slayed these for you, my love. Shall we be wed now?" Nothing says romance like a sack full of crows, am I right?

Now, before you imagine New England suitors desperately chasing crows in full wedding attire, let's set the context. In colonial times, blackbirds and crows were more than just atmospheric creatures from an Edgar Allan Poe poem – they were genuine pests. These birds loved to gobble up crops, especially corn. And corn was life for those early settlers (you don't survive harsh New England winters on clam chowder alone). Towns placed bounties on bird beaks to protect their harvests. Eastham, a neighboring town to Truro, reportedly had an ordinance requiring every household to kill a dozen blackbirds or a few crows each year. Basically, pest control was a civic duty.

Truro apparently decided to get clever (or just absurdly macho about it) with their pest control. They tied the bird-killing quota to bachelorhood. The idea might have been: if you're a single man, you likely have spare time and energy – go help the community by reducing the bird population. Oh, you want to get married and presumably start focusing on, you know, your wife and kids instead of shooting birds at dawn? Fine – but do your quota *first*. In essence: no marriage until you've proven you can provide... by providing a heap of dead blackbirds. It's like the strangest engagement scavenger hunt ever conceived.

Imagine the courting rituals under this law. A young man, eager to propose, heads out with his musket or slingshot and won't come back until he's got the required avian body count. Perhaps he kneels before his beloved, not with a ring, but with a string of blackbird carcasses: "Sweetheart, I have fulfilled the town's requirement. Will you marry me now (before they ask me to bring a dozen squirrels too)?" One hopes the bride-to-be was *very* understanding. "Oh darling, you shouldn't have! Six blackbirds? You really do care!" If that doesn't warm the heart, I don't know what will.

And consider the poor clerks who had to enforce this rule. "Congratulations on your engagement, Jedediah. Now, where are your birds?" Did bachelors show up with a sack over one shoulder, like some morbid Santa delivering feathery proof of eligibility? Maybe there was even a competition among suitors: "I got my six blackbirds in an hour!" "Oh yeah? I bagged three crows before breakfast. Get on my level, bro." It's the colonial version of bragging about your bench press at the gym. The more blackbirds you bag, the more *manly* (and marriageable) you are.

Of course, if Hollywood rom-coms have taught us anything, it's that any obstacle to marriage can be spun into a dramatic twist. Cue a scene where the heroine's father grumbles, "That boy must kill six blackbirds to earn your hand!" And the city-slicker boyfriend, who's never harmed a fly, must bumble through cranberry bogs in a slapstick montage to prove his love. Frankly, I smell a reboot of *The Hunger Games*, but for weddings: "May the odds be ever in your favor, and may your aim be true, oh eligible bachelors of Truro." Instead of a rose, you get a crow's foot. Romantic.

Interestingly, a famous writer (Henry David Thoreau, of *Walden* fame) once noted this law in a journal, wryly observing that despite the ordinance, the cornfields were still full of pesky blackbirds. He mused that either "many men were not married, or many blackbirds were." In other words, maybe a lot of guys dragged their feet on the bird-killing, staying single longer than they intended – or perhaps they cheated and just *said* they did it. (What's the colonial equivalent of hiring someone on Fiverr? Convince an already-married buddy to "lend" you six bird carcasses? That's friendship right there.)

By today's standards, this law is bonkers, not to mention a bit disturbing (poor birds!). Also, not exactly in line with modern wildlife conservation – imagine PETA's reaction if a town tried this now. We'd have *The Birds 2: Legal Boogaloo* protests. Thankfully, this requirement fluttered into the history books long ago. But it does give us a window into how *pragmatic* marriage laws could be. Forget love – can you keep the crops safe? Can you put food on the table (or at least keep the crows from eating it)? Prove it, then you get a wedding.

On the bright side, perhaps it forged stronger marriages? ("He's a good provider – why, he killed six blackbirds just to marry me!" "Oh my, hold out for a man who can do crows, dear.") Or maybe it was early mother-in-law insurance of a different kind: "I don't care if he's handsome, Martha, can he aim a rifle? Town ordinance says we need a marksman, not a poet!" Practical folk, those colonials.

As absurd as it was, the "fowl requirement" does carry a strange underlying truth: marriage has often come with social expectations and odd hoops to jump through. From dowries to blood tests, humanity has always loved making engaged couples check some boxes. But Truro's bird mandate takes the wedding cake (or should we say pie – blackbird pie, anyone?). It's literally a law for the birds.

So next time you grumble about the hoops modern weddings make you jump (the expense, the guest list drama, the perfect Instagram hashtag), be grateful you're not out in a field with a musket trying to plug six crafty blackbirds. Compared to that, addressing 200 invites or negotiating table arrangements with your future mother-in-law is a *piece of cake*. (Blackbird cake? No thanks.)

Marriage Lesson: Every relationship requires some sacrifice, but let's hope your path to the altar doesn't involve actual hunting and gathering. True love might ask for a heart or a ring – but if it asks for six dead birds, you might want to rethink the red flags!

Denture Disclosure – An old Vermont law made it illegal for a wife to get false teeth without her husband's written permission (toothless grin and bear it)

Our final stop on this journey through marital absurdity takes us to Vermont, where love may be eternal but teeth, sadly, are not. Once upon a time, an old Vermont law declared that a wife could not pop in a set of false teeth without getting written permission from her husband. Yes, you read that correctly: *wifely dentures required hubby's sign-off.* If this law were still enforced today, I suspect a lot more Vermont men would be getting mysteriously elbowed in the mouth at night – "Oops, honey, I accidentally knocked out your teeth. Now neither of us can chew, how about that permission slip?"

To understand how on earth this came to be, we need to step into the way-back machine to the 19th century. Around the 1850s, dentures (then often called "plates" of teeth) were a pricey newfangled thing – think cutting-edge tech, like the smartphones of their day but for your mouth. One apocryphal story behind this law involves a certain Mr. Gilman and his wife. Allegedly, Mr. Gilman was ordered by a court to pay for a set of "mineral teeth" for Mrs. Gilman – perhaps because her natural chompers had gone the way of the dodo, and hubby dearest had the funds. Ol' Gilman was likely not thrilled about this mandatory denture subsidy, so rumor has it he lobbied the Vermont legislature harder than an orthodontist at a taffy convention.

The result? A law saying, essentially, "*Ladies, no getting your choppers replaced without your man's OK.*" In patriarchal logic: if *he's* footing the bill (literally, paying through the tooth), he should have a say. Heaven forbid a grown woman in 1856 decide she wants to chew her food without her husband's blessing!

It's hard to overstate how *insulting* and absurd this is on every level. Not only does it treat women like children needing a permission slip ("Dear Teacher, please allow my wife to have teeth. Signed, Husband."), but it's also oddly specific. Why teeth? Why not haircuts or eyeglasses? One theory: false teeth were expensive luxuries at first, and a miserly husband didn't want wifey spending "his" money on frivolities like, um, being able to chew. So he'd rather she gum her way through life unless he decreed otherwise. Another theory: maybe it was about vanity – some grump decided that a woman shouldn't get to improve her smile unless her spouse agrees. (Did early Vermont have a rash of renegade wives running off to secret denturists for illicit ivory dentures, coming home with a suddenly perfect smile and shocking poor hubby? The scandal!)

Whatever the impetus, the law did exist, tucked away in the dusty annals of Vermont's statutes for years. It's the kind of thing that makes you shake your head and perhaps hold your jaw protectively. If marriage is about supporting each other "in sickness and in health," you'd think missing teeth might count as a health issue to be supportive about. Instead, Vermont basically said, "Not so fast, lady – better get your man's John Hancock before you get those pearly *faux* whites."

Now, it's easy (and fun) to lampoon this as prime evidence of antiquated patriarchy – which it is – but I like to imagine the social scenarios it created. Envision a Vermont dentist in the late 1800s, about to fit Mrs. Smith for a new set of dentures. He pauses: "Ma'am, do you have the permission form? No? I'm sorry, the law's the law. Maybe you can come back with your husband's note. In the meantime, might I suggest soup?" Mrs. Smith, toothless and furious, goes home to Bob. "Bob, sign this darn paper so I can eat solid food again!" Bob, perhaps worried that a new smile will make her too uppity, grumbles and delays. Honestly, it's amazing there aren't recorded instances of Vermont wives whacking their husbands with rolling pins in front of the notary public to expedite the process.

From a modern perspective, this law is both hilarious and horrifying. Hilarious because of its pettiness – of all the things to regulate in a marriage, dental prosthetics?! – and horrifying because it underscores how little agency married women had over their own bodies and health decisions. Your teeth, arguably pretty personal, were legally someone else's business. It adds a new twist to the vow "with all my worldly goods I thee endow" – apparently that included your *dentures*, which legally weren't yours to get without hubby's okay.

Thankfully, this law has long since fallen into disuse (though fun fact: it was never formally repealed in any splashy way, it just kind of… got ignored into oblivion). Dentists in Vermont today are not, I assure you, asking women for a permission slip. If anything, they're asking if you have insurance and reminding you to floss. Modern Vermonters – men and women alike – can laugh about it over a pint of Ben & Jerry's ice cream. (Soft serve, in case you still haven't gotten those dentures. Don't worry, it's Vermont, the ice cream is top-notch and tooth-optional.)

It does leave us with some delightful images and analogies though. Like, what if similar laws existed today? Could you imagine: "In (some state), a wife must obtain her husband's written permission before getting LASIK." Or "Husband must have wife's written permission to shave his beard." Ridiculous, right? Yet, once upon a time, dentures fell into that category. If the stand-up comedians of the 1890s knew about this, they'd have a field day. "Take my wife – to the dentist, please. And don't forget my note giving her permission to open wide!"

In the grand tapestry of weird marriage laws, Vermont's denture dictum is the perfect blend of meddlesome and silly. It didn't spark any epic tales or romantic sagas; rather, it probably sparked a lot of muttered cursing under the breath of toothless wives. But as a concept, it's comedy gold for us. It's the kind of law you cite when your spouse teases you for asking before doing something: "Hey, at least I don't need your written permission to go to the gym… unlike your great-great-grandma needed for her teeth!" One can only hope those great-great-grandpas invariably did the right thing – because if not, they were literally depriving their loved ones of a bite of the wedding cake. And that, dear reader, is just bad manners.

So let's raise a glass (of denture-friendly applesauce) to the progress we've made. Marriage is far from perfect today, but at least it's no longer *legally* toothless. Love should empower, not require a permission slip for self-improvement. And if you want to surprise your spouse with a dazzling new grin, the only signature you need is on the credit card receipt.

Marriage Lesson: In a good marriage, support your partner in all things – including dental health. After all, the couple that *chews* together, stays together. And if you ever feel the urge to control your spouse's smile… bite your tongue, not their rights.

Chapter 9

Happily Never After – Modern Divorce Celebrations and Ceremonies

Divorce used to be spoken of in hushed tones – a sombre epilogue to a story that didn't get its fairy-tale ending. Not anymore! Today, people are turning the end of "happily ever after" into an excuse for cheeky celebration, self-discovery, and even travel. In our irreverent tour of modern divorce traditions, you'll see exes cutting cake, smashing rings, checking in for split-up spa weekends, divorcing themselves (yes, really), and channeling Gwyneth Paltrow vibes as they consciously uncouple. It's marriage's final act done with humor and flair – because if you can't beat 'em, throw a party and *un*join 'em. So grab some confetti and buckle up: this isn't your grandparents' divorce.

Divorce Cakes & Confetti – Celebrating Your Unwedding in Style

Remember when divorce announcements were accompanied by tissues and teary phone calls? Well, now they come with balloons, confetti, and a frosted cake that reads "Happy Divorce." Throwing a divorce party complete with a sassy "unwedding" cake has become a full-on trend, because why should weddings have all the fun? Instead of a shameful secret, a split is just another milestone to fête – a liberation from a toxic or loveless union, worthy of its own dessert buffet. If weddings are about two people starting a life together, divorce parties are about one (or both) of those people getting their life *back*. And what better way to mark the occasion than with cake and champagne among supportive friends?

A three-tier "divorce cake" with a knife-wielding bride and fallen groom topper, served at a celebratory "divorce party" in Las Vegas. Over-the-top confections like this put a sweet spin on the sour end of a marriage, proving you can have your divorce cake and eat it too.

Divorce cakes have evolved into their own cheeky art form. Instead of the dainty bride-and-groom figurine embracing on a wedding cake, you might see a plastic bride kicking a groom off the cake's edge, or a topper where the ex-hubby is literally in the trash can. One famous early example: when Blink-182 drummer Travis Barker split from Shanna Moakler in 2006, she threw a *Vegas* divorce bash complete with a three-tier cake featuring a little bride figurine brandishing a knife over a bloodied groom. (Revenge never tasted so sweet.) That headline-making party – held at the Bellagio, no less – proved that "happily never after" could be an event in itself. It even inspired a nightclub to start offering divorce party packages for the newly single, "celebrating the beginning of their freedom" instead of mourning the end of it. Leave it to Hollywood and Las Vegas to make breaking up as glamourous as getting hitched.

These days, you don't have to be a rockstar's ex to revel in a divorce celebration. Regular folks are hopping on the bandwagon, turning their post-split blues into a red-carpet moment (or at least a rowdy girls' night). At your average divorce party, you'll gather your best buddies – the ones who dragged you through the drama – for a night of laughter, dancing, and maybe a piñata shaped like a heart to smash. The vibe is akin to a bachelorette party in reverse: instead of "So long, single life!" it's "So long, married life!". And yes, there will be cake. As one report describes, these cakes often come with tongue-in-cheek designs and quotes: a bride taking out the trash (guess who's in the garbage can) or frosting that proclaims "Free at Last!". It's common to see celebratory slogans like *"Divorced AF"* or even Ariana Grande lyrics – one bakery offers a "Thank U, Next" cake, turning the pop anthem into a post-marriage mantra. The message is loud and clear: congratulations on your new chapter.

Why throw a party at a time that's normally associated with stress, lawyers, and ugly crying? For one, it flips the script. Instead of viewing divorce as a failure, the divorce-party trend treats it as a rite of passage – the "unwedding" that officially lets you start fresh. Friends and family come not to commiserate but to uplift the newly single individual, offering support (and maybe new kitchenware gifts – divorce registries are a thing now) as they embark on solo life. Psychologists might call it reframing; we'd call it turning lemons into lemon drop shots. "Move over, wedding bells, it's time for freedom bells," as one divorce party planner quipped, likely while hanging a "Just Divorced!" banner. By infusing humor and celebration into a breakup, people reclaim a sense of control and optimism. After all, if you can laugh at a divorce cake depicting your ex's downfall, you're probably going to be OK.

Beyond the gags and booze, there's a kernel of empowerment here. A divorce celebration provides closure and a "toast to new beginnings" in a way a dry court decree can't. It's like an Irish wake for the marriage – mourn a little, but also toast to life continuing. Instead of death do us part, it's death did us part and now we party. Attendees often dress to the nines (some divorcees even dig that old wedding dress out for one more night on the town as a lark). They make speeches not to roast the ex, but to cheer on the divorcé(e)'s freedom and future. It's catharsis through cake and karaoke. One might belt out Gloria Gaynor's *"I Will Survive"* or Taylor Swift's *"We Are Never Ever Getting Back Together"* at full volume, surrounded by smiling friends rather than sitting home alone with a box of tissues. In a culture where *getting* married is applauded, it was only a matter of time before *ending* a marriage – especially a bad one – got its own applause, too.

So yes, the *unhappy* ending has become its own happy event. Divorce parties and their decadent cakes send a bold message: sometimes the end of a marriage is something to celebrate. It's not that divorce isn't painful; it's that you're allowed to find joy and humor even in pain. As one cake decorator mused while crafting a "Legally Single" cake, these celebrations are about "embracing positivity and toasting to new beginnings". In other words, healing can come with a side of buttercream. Happily never after, and proud of it.

Ring Smash Bash – Japan's Formal Divorce Ceremony (Bring Your Own Mallet)

If divorce cakes feel a bit *too* frivolous for your taste, consider Japan's approach – equal parts solemn ritual and absurd pageantry. In the Land of the Rising Divorce, unhappy couples have been holding formal divorce ceremonies, complete with guests, speeches, and the grand finale: smashing their wedding rings with a mighty mallet. Yes, this is a real thing. Think of it as a bizarro wedding: instead of "with this ring, I thee wed," it's *"with this mallet, I thee divorce."* Crunch!

The divorce ceremony trend in Japan was pioneered by a self-styled "divorce planner" named Hiroki Terai, who basically said, "People have a ceremony when they get married, so why not for divorces, too?". Why not indeed. Terai's services provide soon-to-be-ex spouses a chance to ritually unravel their union in front of an audience. It's half group-therapy, half theater, with Terai officiating like an anti-priest. One typical ceremony might begin with the estranged husband and wife arriving in style – in separate rickshaws, no less – processing slowly through the streets of Tokyo as if en route to a funeral. (In a sense, it *is* a funeral: the funeral of the marriage.) Friends and family walk behind in respectful silence, eyes down. The atmosphere is somber and surreal. If you didn't know better, you'd think they were headed to a last rites ritual – which, metaphorically, they are.

Terai often chooses a rundown "divorce mansion" (actually a humble rented space or even a parking garage) as the venue, deliberately shabby to reflect the relationship's disintegration. No five-star wedding ballroom here – peeling paint and concrete floors set the mood. The ceremony proceeds with opening remarks where the planner tactfully recounts why the couple is splitting (sanitized for the crowd: no airing of dirty laundry, just a vague "they drifted apart"). There may even be a slideshow of the couple's happier times (yes, some packages offer a divorce slideshow – equal parts touching and twisted). Then comes a brief toast. But instead of raising champagne flutes, everyone raises cups of green tea – in one ceremony, they explicitly toasted with tea to avoid *"alcohol-fuelled"* outbursts or truth-telling tirades. No one wants Uncle Kenji heckling the exes after one too many sakés, after all.

Finally, it's time for the pièce de résistance: the ring smash bash. The nearly-divorced duo joins hands on a wooden mallet, and with their guests looking on, they smash their wedding ring to smithereens on a little anvil. *Wham!* With one (or two) hefty thuds – sometimes it takes a couple of tries to really squish that sucker – the symbolic band of matrimony is flattened into a sad metal pancake. Talk about catharsis! The audience offers polite, half-hearted applause as the deed is done. The once-betrothed couple has literally broken the last tangible link of their union. If a Western divorce is about signing papers, a Japanese divorce ceremony is about crushing the past – quite literally – in front of witnesses. It's dramatic, a little awkward, but undeniably satisfying if you're into that sort of thing.

A couple in Tokyo uses a mallet to smash their wedding ring during a formal "divorce ceremony," symbolically ending their marriage. The mallet and frog-shaped receptacle (yes, that's a frog) are part of the ritual – in Japanese, "frog" (kaeru) sounds like "change," signaling a leap into a new life.

In true quirky fashion, Terai infuses the ritual with a bit of playful symbolism: the mallet used for ring-smashing is often adorned with a frog's head, and a pink frog-shaped statue gobbles up the mangled ring bits. Why a frog? Because in Japanese, the word for frog (*kaeru*) is a homonym for "to change" or "to return." The idea is that the couple is changing back into single individuals – shedding their married selves like amphibians molting skin. It's basically a fairy tale in reverse: instead of kissing a frog to get a prince, the princess takes a frog hammer and bludgeons the ring to be rid of her prince. How's that for closure? Mr. Terai explains that many participants, even those initially hesitant, are surprised by how happy and relieved they feel when that hammer comes down. One divorcee described the act by saying *"I could see the future ahead of me for the first time. It was like being reset to zero."* In other words, nothing says fresh start like smashing your old life into metallic scrap and feeding it to a frog.

These ceremonies have grown from a niche offering to a mini-industry. Terai's half-day "divorce tour" costs around ¥55,000 (about $600) and has attracted hundreds of inquiries since 2009. Sometimes they even host larger divorce ceremonies in hotel banquet halls – the same places that normally host wedding receptions, just repurposed for untying the knot. The irony is rich: Saturday morning, one couple might cut a wedding cake in that hall; by Saturday evening, another couple is smashing a ring in the very same room. As Terai notes, Japanese culture has ceremonies for both beginnings and endings – so why should marriage be an exception? What he offers is a final milestone to mark the end of a journey. It's less "Game Over" and more "mission accomplished, time to move on." Guests who attended the couple's wedding sometimes attend the divorce ceremony too – a symmetry that could be either touching or a tad cruel, depending on your perspective (imagine Aunt Keiko whispering, "Well, at least the divorce buffet has sushi *and* cake").

Western onlookers often find this divorce-ceremony trend bizarre, but even skeptics admit there's a certain appeal. It makes the split tangible and maybe a bit more amiable. Rather than slink off to sign papers in a dreary office, couples here publicly acknowledge the end of their marriage with ritual and respect – and maybe a touch of dark humor. As one commentator noted, these ceremonies end the marriage "in a way that is amicable, rather than acrimonious". Sure, it's quirky – some might say *extra* – but if it helps exes achieve closure, more power (and mallets) to them. Compared to the average divorce court showdown, a ring smash bash seems positively civil. Perhaps the rest of the world could learn something from this: sometimes a clean break *literally* requires a hammer. Just be sure to watch your fingers.

Weekend Divorce Getaway – Checking In Married, Checking Out Single (No Room Service Included)

If ritual ring-smashing feels too quaint and you'd prefer to expedite your uncoupling in luxury, then pack your bags for the Divorce Hotel. Yes, you read that right – a hotel for divorcing. Think of it as a twisted romantic weekend: you and your soon-to-be-ex check in on Friday as a married couple, and check out by Sunday as happily (never) after singles. It's a real offering that started in the Netherlands – a country already famous for tulips and tolerant attitudes, now also a pioneer in concierge divorce. The idea is to make splitting up as *efficient* as a Vegas drive-thru wedding chapel, but with a high-end, spa-like twist. You get a comfortable suite, a team of mediators and lawyers on call, and 48 hours to negotiate every last detail of your separation. By the end of the weekend, if all goes well, you walk out with your divorce agreement finalized – and maybe treat yourself to a massage or a stiff drink at the hotel bar to celebrate the successful breakup.

The concept was the brainchild of Dutch entrepreneur Jim Halfens, who clearly saw gold in them thar marital ruins. "Quickie divorce, luxury setting" is the basic pitch. On Friday, you're greeted at a nice hotel (initially a boutique property in the Netherlands, but the idea proved so catchy it even expanded to places like the upscale Gideon Putnam Resort in New York). Instead of bellhops and honeymoon suites, you're ushered into a conference room with legal professionals. Over the next two days, you and your spouse-in-transition meet with mediators, lawyers, financial planners – basically a divorce SWAT team – to hammer out asset divisions, custody arrangements, and who gets the dog. It's intense but contained: rather than dragging on for months, the whole process is compressed into one power weekend in a neutral, plush environment. By Sunday, paperwork is prepared for filing, and you've essentially done the divorce equivalent of ripping off the Band-Aid. As one description summed it up, *"On a Friday, a couple checks into a designated luxury hotel… On Monday, after meeting with lawyers, mediators, notaries, and psychologists all weekend, the pair walks away amicably, with divorce papers signed, for one flat fee."* All of the pain, half the time – and you get pillow mints to boot.

The flat fee, by the way, ranges from roughly $3,000 to $10,000 for the weekend package. At first that sticker price might induce a spit-take – who knew breaking up could cost as much as a deluxe vacation? But compared to drawn-out litigation (which can rack up tens of thousands in legal bills), a Divorce Hotel stay could actually be a bargain. It's the Groupon of dissolutions! Of course, the price assumes you and your ex can behave like adults for two days. In fact, not every couple is eligible. The Divorce Hotel team vets applicants to ensure both parties are truly willing to negotiate peacefully. "We can't split up everybody," Halfens admitted; if a duo shows up seething with rage or acting "childish," they get sent to the traditional courtroom route. In other words, if you're planning to reenact *War of the Roses*, you won't make it past check-in. The service is aimed at couples who have mutually decided to part and just want to get it over with quickly – preferably without any vases thrown or tires slashed in the process.

What's fascinating (and a little hilarious) is how the whole experience is framed with almost honeymoon-like serenity. One promo promised the weekend would be "professional, fast, affordable and hopefully positive" – as if you might leave *glowing* after divvying up the house and 401(k). The hotel setting helps set a civil tone: you're on neutral ground, in quiet luxury, maybe enjoying a walk on the hotel grounds between mediation sessions. There's room service (though probably not included in the divorce package price), fluffy robes, and a spa on site in case you need to unwind after discussing who gets the cat. It's divorce, but make it vacation. One American commentator quipped it sounded like a DIY spa treatment for breakups – an *"idyllic"* weekend of sipping peach bellinis on the balcony after signing a custody plan. (Sign here, then relax by the pool – not a bad deal.) Of course, reality TV came knocking: a Dutch reality show was made about the concept, and pilots were shot for an American version too. Because what's more binge-worthy than watching couples negotiate alimony at a resort? Imagine *Survivor*, but both contestants win by splitting the prize – literally.

Even celebrities were intrigued. Back when Demi Moore and Ashton Kutcher's high-profile marriage was on the rocks, they were reportedly invited to try the Divorce Hotel program as VIP guinea pigs. (They declined – perhaps realizing that a private mediated weekend beats a public circus, or maybe because *Two and a Half Men* royalties can fund a more bespoke divorce plan.) Still, the very idea of jet-setting to a resort to end your union caught the world's attention. It speaks to a broader cultural shift: divorce doesn't have to equal drama; it can be a civil, even dignified, transaction. Why not handle it like a business retreat? Check in, have a few productive meetings, sign on the dotted line, and part with a handshake – and maybe a mimosa toast to your respective futures. If that sounds a tad optimistic, well, the Dutch are known for pragmatism. One might even say this approach gives "getting suite revenge" a whole new meaning.

Of course, not everyone's divorce can be handled in 48 hours at the Marriott. But the existence of Divorce Hotels sends a clear message: the market is answering a demand for kinder, quicker breakups. Millennials and Gen Xers, children of the bitter divorce wars of the '80s and '90s, are seeking a *"good divorce"* – one with minimal collateral damage and maximum efficiency. Why scorch the earth if you can sign the papers and then hit the spa? As one lawyer involved noted, it only works if couples are *keen* to make a clean break. It's divorce for the amicable, or at least the amicably-minded. And while it might sound surreal to enjoy a massage after divvying up assets, hey, stranger things have happened in the realm of matrimony (looking at you, 72-day celebrity marriages).

It's also fun to imagine other applications: perhaps Brexit could have been settled faster if EU and UK negotiators had a Divorce Hotel weekend? Lock Boris Johnson and EU officials in a château with mediators and let them hash out the separation over 48 hours – croissants in the morning, compromise in the afternoon. (One commentator did call Brexit a "conscious uncoupling, not a nasty divorce" – wishful thinking, as it turned out.) Or maybe high-profile billionaire breakups could be handled this way: "Welcome to the Bezos Breakup Resort. Please enjoy our Amazon Gift Shop on your way out." Jokes aside, the fact that we're even talking about divorce getaways means the stigma is fading. A divorce can now be an experience you schedule and get done, like removing a bandaid – maybe not fun, but mercifully quick.

In the end, whether you opt for a dramatic ring smash or a chill weekend of paperwork and spa robes, the goal is the same: get through a painful process with less pain (and okay, maybe a nifty story to tell afterward). The Divorce Hotel is essentially Marie Kondo-ing a marriage – thanking it for its lessons, then swiftly tidying it away. And if you check out with a nicely sorted life and no loose ends (except that one left-behind toothbrush), that's worth a five-star review.

Sologamy Self-Split – When You Divorce… Yourself (The Ultimate It's-Not-You-It's-Me)

As if modern love couldn't get more avant-garde, allow us to introduce a plot twist straight out of a Black Mirror rom-com: sologamy, the act of marrying oneself – and its inevitable counterpart, divorcing oneself. Yes, the *self*-love journey can come full circle, ending not with "happily ever after" but "happily never after" to *oneself.* Case in point: a Brazilian influencer named Suellen Carey made global headlines by marrying herself in 2023 as a flamboyant declaration of independence and self-love. Dressed in a wedding gown, she vowed to honor and cherish herself; she threw the bouquet to, well, herself; she probably even had a first dance solo. It was the ultimate statement that she didn't need anybody else to be happy. But fast forward one year, and guess what? She filed for divorce…from herself. If your jaw just dropped, you're not alone. It turns out even *solo* weddings can end in heartbreak (or at least in exasperation).

Suellen's self-split wasn't due to infidelity (unless she two-timed herself with Netflix binges, which we doubt) – it was due to the crushing realization that even being your own spouse is hard work. In interviews, she explained that she had set very high expectations of her wedded life with herself – she wanted to be the perfect partner to *herself* – and unsurprisingly, she couldn't live up to those expectations. (Talk about a toxic relationship; she literally couldn't please herself!) She admitted she often felt lonely *with herself* and even exhausted, as if she were putting too much pressure on the "marriage" to succeed. The situation sounds like a comedy sketch: *"It's not you, it's… well, actually it IS me. I just can't do this anymore."* She tried to make it work – notably by going to couples therapy alone. Yes, imagine sitting in a therapist's office doing exercises like "Active Listening," where you as the husband listen to you as the wife. Suellen actually went through 10 therapy sessions in an attempt to save her solo marriage. That's dedication – or perhaps the very definition of splitting your personality. In the end, after much self-reflection (literally), she concluded that divorce was the healthiest option. "Even in a marriage with ourselves, it's important to accept our imperfections," she wisely noted, explaining that she'd been *"putting a lot of pressure on myself and that sometimes left me exhausted."*. The self-wife was just *over* her self-husband, apparently.

The tale of the sologamist divorcee is equal parts poignant and absurd – a perfect parable for our narcissistic times. It's easy to poke fun ("She and herself just weren't compatible – irreconcilable similarities"), but there's also a human truth in it. Marrying yourself, beyond the clickbait headline, was meant to be a message about self-love and not settling for less than you deserve. Yet even that experiment revealed something: no man (or woman) is an island. Humans are social creatures, and maybe we aren't meant to be both partners in a marriage. Being your own everything can get lonely, shockingly enough. Suellen found that out the hard way. She said that despite initially enjoying her symbolic solo union, eventually *"dissatisfaction and loneliness"* crept in. She missed, well, other people. Who do you binge Netflix with when you're your own spouse? Who do you blame when the toilet seat is left up (answer: still yourself, darn it!)? The honeymoon with oneself can only last so long before reality sets in – there is no *other* to share life's duties and joys. Even making dinner, you can't be pleasantly surprised by your partner's cooking; it's just you again, ordering pizza for one. Self-marriage, it appears, had all the same challenges of a regular marriage – communication issues (do you give yourself the silent treatment?), unmet expectations, and the danger of taking your partner (you) for granted.

To Suellen's credit, she doesn't regret her sologamy. She called it a valuable process of "self-discovery" and healing, one that taught her to prioritize her own well-being. In a poetic twist, divorcing herself was the final act of that self-discovery – realizing that loving yourself sometimes means not *shackling* yourself. And in a happy epilogue, she's now open to finding an actual partner "to share new experiences" with. In other words, Ms. Right is now looking for Mr. Right, having already been Ms. *Always Right* in her previous "marriage." The internet had a field day with her story – cue the jokes about "irreconcilable differences with my better half (me)" and "custody battle over the cats with myself." But beyond the punchlines, there's an oddly uplifting takeaway: you've got to truly love yourself before you can love someone else, but also, loving yourself doesn't mean you have to literally *marry* yourself. Self-love is healthy; self-marriage, it turns out, is a bit redundant (and paperwork-intensive – imagine serving divorce papers to yourself).

Interestingly, Suellen's isn't the only sologamy story out there. Others have attempted it – a British woman married herself in a full ceremony; a Japanese man married a hologram (that's a whole other level of "it's just me and my imagination"). One Brazilian model, Cris Galêra, married herself and then divorced in mere months because she met someone special – apparently Prince Charming showed up *right after* she put a ring on *her own* finger. You can't make this stuff up. It's a reminder that love is strange and there are no limits to human creativity (or perhaps desperation) in matters of the heart. If marriage is a mirror, sologamy is a mirror that talks back – and sometimes, as Suellen learned, it says, "I need some space... from myself."

As humorous as it is, the self-divorce saga of Suellen Carey yields a modern moral: self-partnership is nice, but it's okay to admit you still want partnership with another actual person. It also proves that no relationship is without its challenges – even the one you have with *you*. In an era of "you complete me" being replaced with "I complete myself," we've discovered that even the completely complete can feel incomplete. So if you ever find yourself single and considering marrying yourself for the Instagram likes, remember that you might end up having a very awkward conversation a year later: "Self, we need to talk..." And when you tell yourself "I think we should see other people," you'll finally be taking your own advice.

Conscious Uncoupling – Splitting with Gwyneth Paltrow Spa Vibes (Goop-y Breakups)

Leave it to Hollywood to rebrand a breakup as something spiritual and enlightened. When actress-turned-lifestyle-guru Gwyneth Paltrow announced her split from Coldplay frontman Chris Martin in 2014, she infamously dubbed it a "conscious uncoupling." The world collectively scratched its head – and rolled its eyes. To many, it sounded like a pretentious way of saying "We're getting divorced," as if the couple were two celestial beings calmly parting ways in a yoga studio. Critics joked that Paltrow made one of life's most stressful events sound like a DIY spa treatment. (One snarky headline read: *"Conscious Uncoupling? I unconsciously uncoupled and didn't even realize it."*) How dare she apply aromatherapy and zen platitudes to something as messy as divorce! And yet, a decade later, "conscious uncoupling" has entered the zeitgeist – even the dictionary – as a term for splitting on good terms. It's the Goopification of divorce, complete with scented candles and healing crystals. Breakups, Paltrow-style, come with a side of kale smoothie and personal growth.

So what *is* conscious uncoupling, beyond the buzzword? The phrase was coined by therapist Katherine Woodward Thomas, but Gwyneth gave it fame. It's essentially the idea of ending a relationship with intention, mutual respect, and minimal damage – treating the divorce not as a failure, but as a *transformation*. Instead of mud-slinging and winner-takes-all legal battles, the conscious uncouplers strive to remain friends, co-parent harmoniously, and maybe even do meditation retreats together. Paltrow and Martin's announcement on Goop (her wellness website) insisted they were *"closer than we have ever been"* even as they decided to separate. They framed it like a journey of growth, emphasizing love and family, just no longer *marriage*. It read a bit like a Hallmark card mixed with a self-help manual: lovingly complete the relationship and remain whole and at peace. In fact, Woodward Thomas describes conscious uncoupling as *"a proven process for lovingly completing a relationship that will leave you feeling whole and healed and at peace."* All that's missing is a hot stone massage and some whale music in the background.

The public reaction back in 2014 was, to put it mildly, derisive. People called it out as an absurd euphemism – "conscious uncoupling" sounded like what happens when you untangle headphone wires, not a heart-wrenching split. Late-night comedians had a field day. But here's the kicker: Paltrow may have been ahead of her time. In recent years, more and more couples (famous and not) are aiming for that amicable split ideal. The term "good divorce" is no longer an oxymoron. Millennials, in particular, seem determined to divorce *better* than their parents did – less drama, more collaboration. They're the generation that will invite the ex-spouse to Thanksgiving dinner for the sake of the kids (and Instagram). Gwyneth just gave them a fancy term and a template. By now, conscious uncoupling even has a certain chicness to it. It's been referenced in TV shows, think-pieces, and yes, as a joking analogy for political separations. (During Brexit, some optimists suggested the UK and EU could consciously uncouple; realists noted it was more like an old-fashioned bitter divorce with crockery thrown – one columnist wrote, *"Forget Gwyneth Paltrow's idea of conscious uncoupling. This will be anger, rancour and tears."* Spoiler: they were right.)

What does a conscious uncoupling look like in practice? Picture a couple doing yoga breathing exercises as they calmly discuss dividing assets. Perhaps they hold a small ceremony to "release" each other, exchanging gratitude for the years spent together. They might even take a final family vacation – Gwyneth and Chris famously went on holiday together in the midst of divorcing, to show unity for the kids (and probably to prove to the world how evolved they were). No lawyers leaking dirt to TMZ, no courtroom showdowns – just two beautiful people having a beautifully orchestrated split. It's divorce with a spa-day glow. One reporter quipped that Paltrow made divorce sound like a *"kinder, gentler way to dissolve a marriage – simply put, a good divorce."* Skeptics gagged, but plenty of folks quietly thought, "I'll have what she's having."

And indeed, some other celebs have followed suit in rebranding their breakups. Take rock star Jack White and model Karen Elson: they threw a divorce party together in 2011, celebrating both their 6th wedding anniversary and impending split in one fell swoop – invitations even described it as a positive celebration of their time together. That's conscious uncoupling with a rock 'n' roll twist (and perhaps a keg). Or consider actors Anna Faris and Chris Pratt, who managed to gush publicly about each other even as they divorced, emphasizing friendship and respect. Even mega-billionaires Bill and Melinda Gates managed a drama-free divorce, releasing statements about continued cooperation on philanthropy – basically a corporate version of conscious uncoupling where the only casualty was a $130 billion redistribution. It's as if Gwyneth whispered to the culture: *"You can break up nicely, darlings,"* and some actually listened.

Of course, we must acknowledge the elephant in the room: conscious uncoupling can come off as ridiculously privileged. It helps when you're rich, famous, and have access to couples' counselors, mindfulness gurus, and an army of PR agents to spin your split into gold. For regular folks, maintaining that level of serenity while untangling a shared life is challenging to say the least. Most exes don't have the luxury of a private island vacation to bond post-breakup or a Goop pop-up kit for emotional detox. Sometimes, you just want to key your ex's car – not lovingly thank them for the lessons learned. But the aspirational ideal is out there now. Even if we laugh at the phrasing, the core idea – end a relationship with empathy instead of bitterness – is something many can get behind. It's essentially marriage therapy values carried through to the divorce: communicate, forgive, move forward whole. It's hard to argue with that goal (even if the Goop-y jargon triggers your gag reflex).

Gwyneth Paltrow herself has leaned fully into the concept. Years later, she mused that she was proud to have coined a term that "redefined divorce in the 21st century" – a bit self-congratulatory, but not entirely untrue. "Conscious uncoupling" has entered the modern lexicon, and even if people use it tongue-in-cheek, it reflects an evolution in how we view breakups. It's no longer mandatory to pick sides and assume divorcing couples despise each other. Some truly do sail into the sunset as friends. (Not all, but some – we're not in utopia yet.) The term also encourages separating couples to be, well, *conscious* – to think about the impact on kids, on each other, and to actively choose a respectful route over a scorched-earth one. In a way, it's the polar opposite of those dramatic divorce traditions we saw earlier. If the Japanese ring-smash is about catharsis through destruction, conscious uncoupling is about healing through gentleness. If the divorce party is about gleeful liberation, conscious uncoupling is about solemn gratitude. Different strokes for different folks – one size does *not* fit all when it comes to breaking up.

So, what marriage lessons can we glean from this smorgasbord of modern divorce trends? For one: people are resilient and endlessly inventive in finding meaning (or at least coping mechanisms) in heartbreak. Whether it's slicing up a "Happy Divorce" cake, pulverizing a ring, fast-tracking the split at a Divorce Hotel, divorcing your own darn self, or slapping a wellness buzzword on the whole ordeal – the end of a marriage is no longer seen as just a tragedy. It can be a transition, even a transformation, to navigate with style or humor. Perhaps the biggest lesson is that how a relationship *ends* can be just as telling as how it began. Each of these trends carries an insight: celebrating a divorce highlights the courage in choosing happiness over convention; ritualizing a divorce acknowledges the emotional importance of closure; streamlining a divorce shows that pragmatism and peace often beat drawn-out vengeance; even a self-divorce teaches that every relationship (including the one with yourself) takes care and honesty; and conscious uncoupling reminds us that endings can be handled with kindness and dignity.

At the end of the day – or chapter, as it were – "happily never after" might not be such a bad thing. It might mean happier apart, a second chance at joy, or simply relief and recovery. Modern divorce ceremonies and celebrations, in all their quirky glory, are society's way of saying: *Life doesn't always go according to plan, but we can still celebrate moving forward.* As irreverent as some of these practices are (pass the mallet, would you?), they all underscore a cultural shift:

divorce is not a taboo failure to be hidden in the shadows; it's a reality that many face, and increasingly, face with head held high – perhaps while wearing a "Just Divorced" tiara and tossing confetti. So here's to the odd, empowering, funny ways people say goodbye to matrimony. In the game of love, not everyone wins forever – but you can still throw one heck of a going-away party for your marriage. And who knows? You just might find that the end is, in fact, a beginning in disguise – one worth toasting with a slice of liberating cake and maybe a conscious champagne uncoupling. Cheers to happily never after!

Chapter 10

Stranger Than Fiction – The Bizarrest Odds and Ends of 'I Do' and 'I Don't'

Raining Cats, Frogs, and Goats – In parts of India, people have married frogs, dogs, even donkeys in elaborate ceremonies to ward off curses or summon rain

Grab your umbrella (and maybe a wedding gift), because in some parts of the world, "raining cats and dogs" isn't just an idiom – it's a *wedding strategy*. Imagine a drought-stricken village where the crops are wilting, the wells are drying up, and the local rainmaker is sending all calls to voicemail. What's the solution? Why, a big, fat amphibian wedding, of course! In rural India, it's not unheard of to see two frogs get hitched in a full-blown ceremony – baraat (wedding procession), priestly blessings, tiny froggy outfits, and all – with the hope that the rain gods will RSVP "Yes" and shower the region with monsoon bliss. It's like a rain dance, but with vows and lily pads. And believe it or not, these frog weddings have *worked* a little *too* well on occasion: one celebrated frog couple in Madhya Pradesh was quickly "divorced" when their honeymoon coincided with flood-inducing downpours. Till rain do us part, indeed.

Frogs aren't the only creatures hopping down the aisle. In the quest to appease the heavens (or sometimes to lift a local curse), weddings for dogs, donkeys, and other critters have also made the guest list. Villagers in Assam and Maharashtra have merrily married off frogs during droughts, while one Tamil Nadu community decided that two donkeys tying the knot would do the trick to end a dry spell. Picture that: a bride and groom who both have the hee-haws. The donkeys were decked out in floral garlands, trotting around as the crowd cheered – essentially the equine version of *My Big Fat Indian Wedding.* There were priests chanting mantras for the donkey bride and groom, likely wondering in the back of their minds if they missed a memo from the Almighty on this one. If anyone objected to the union, perhaps a loud *"EE-AW!"* was the only protest, quickly overruled by the promise of rainfall. And you thought Vegas chapel weddings were wild!

Why stop at frogs and donkeys? Dogs have entered the matrimonial mix too (though we'll get to one very special canine case in the next section). In some instances, children born under certain "cursed" astrological conditions – say, a bad horoscope or a pesky evil eye – are *remedied* by symbolically marrying them off to an animal first. The logic (if you can call it that) is that the curse gets tricked or transferred to the animal spouse, freeing the human for a future "real" marriage with a fellow human. For example, a girl might be ceremonially married to a stray dog in an elaborate rite to ward off an ominous prediction that her eventual human husband might die young. The dog, presumably, does not mind being a temporary stand-in groom as long as there are treats involved. The community celebrates, the curse is considered placated, and the girl is now safe to marry the man of her dreams without any spectral baggage – while the dog groom happily returns to bachelor life, tail wagging.

These animal weddings are often extravagant community affairs, equal parts heartfelt and head-scratching. There's music, dancing, and feasting – a joyous gathering with an utterly bizarre centerpiece. You can almost imagine the conversations among guests: "So, how do you know the bride?" – "Oh, I went to obedience school with her." *Ba-dum-tss!* It's the kind of scene that would make Dr. Dolittle spit out his tea. Yet, behind the absurdity lies a kind of earnest hope. In dire times – whether it's a drought or a run of bad luck – people grasp at any tradition that might set things right, even if it means throwing a wedding for a couple of croaking lovebirds (er, lovefrogs). It's a quirky mix of faith and folklore: if you can't beat the weather, trick it with a wedding.

At the end of the day (hopefully with a rainbow overhead), these oddball nuptials provide plenty of laughs for outsiders and perhaps a sigh of relief for participants. Skeptics roll their eyes, scientists facepalm, and the newly-"wed" frogs? They just kind of blink and flick their tongues, blissfully unaware that they're now married in the eyes of villagers and gods. It's a story so strange, if you saw it in a satirical movie you'd chuckle and say, "Nah, that would never happen in real life." Surprise – it does! And it's only the tip of the iceberg when it comes to the bizarre lengths people will go for a happily-ever-after (or at least a change in the weather).

Marriage Lesson: When life gives you a drought, throw a wedding – sometimes a leap of faith (or a hop of a frog) is the ultimate rain dance.

The Cursed Canine Groom – An Indian man once wed a dog to atone for killing two dogs years prior – a priest and 200 guests attended the ceremony to lift his "mutt" curse

They say every dog has its day, but one man in India took that adage to a whole new level – *by making a dog his bride for a day*. Yes, you read that correctly. In perhaps the most bizarre "love story" ever told, a 33-year-old man named Selvakumar showed up at the altar in Tamil Nadu with a nervous smile and a female stray dog named Selvi by his side, both decked out in wedding finery. No, this wasn't some avant-garde take on "man's best friend" or a PETA publicity stunt. It was an act of atonement. Years earlier, Selvakumar had committed a dreadful deed – he'd stoned two dogs to death (a heinous act that presumably put him on *Cujo's* hit list for life). Not long after, according to him, karma came a-knockin'. He began suffering mysterious paralysis in his legs and partial hearing loss. Doctors were baffled, but the village elders and astrologers nodded knowingly: *curse of the vengeful canine spirits.* The solution? A wedding. Obviously.

And so, our guilt-ridden groom did what any reasonable person would do when cursed by ghost dogs – he married a dog in a lavish ceremony to break the curse. It sounds like a plot straight out of a Monty Python skit or an Onion headline: *"Man Marries Dog to Lift Mutt Curse; Hopes Life Will Stop Being Ruff."* But for Selvakumar, this was deadly serious (well, maybe not deadly – the whole point was to *avoid* that). The big day arrived with all the pomp of a traditional Hindu wedding. Selvi the dog was bathed, draped in a silky orange sari, and adorned with a flower garland. One imagines she might have preferred a nice collar and a chew toy, but hey, when in Rome – or in this case, when in Tamil Nadu – you do as the village astrologer says.

A priest chanted Sanskrit prayers, likely doing a double-take each time he glanced at the "bride." Vows were pronounced (the groom said "I do," the dog presumably said "Woof"), and Selvakumar placed a bridal garland around Selvi's neck with trembling hands – hopefully from nerves, not lingering paralysis. Over 200 guests gathered to bless this most *unusual* union, many dressed in their Sunday best, because how often do you get to attend a dog's wedding? Villagers cheered, children giggled, and local reporters had a field day. After the ceremony, the newlyweds sat down to a wedding feast. The groom and his human relatives enjoyed a traditional meal (perhaps avoiding hot dogs out of respect), while the canine bride was treated to a bun and plenty of petting. If there was a wedding cake, one assumes Selvi got first dibs at the icing.

The images from that day are equal parts heartwarming and head-scratching: a man genuinely smiling in relief as he kneels beside a bewildered-looking dog in a sari. Selvakumar believed wholeheartedly that this act of matrimonial penance would appease the spirits of the dogs he'd wronged and lift his torment. In a way, it's a story of redemption – extremely weird, tail-wagging redemption. It gives a whole new meaning to *"dogged determination to fix one's mistakes."* While we don't know for sure if Selvakumar's health improved afterward (the news reports were frustratingly silent on the *medical* efficacy of marrying a dog), one can only hope the curse was broken and he didn't have to resort to marrying, say, a cat next. Selvi, for her part, was a free dog after the ceremony – no honeymoon needed, and absolutely no consummation (let's be clear, this was purely symbolic holy muttrimony).

It's easy to poke fun at the sheer absurdity of it all. (Trust me, my inner comedian is doing cartwheels: "Talk about a ruff marriage," "That's one way to get apaw-tnership," and so on.) But there's also something oddly touching about a community coming together to support one man's quest for forgiveness – even if that quest involves a four-legged fiancée. In attendance were likely the same people who had whispered about his "curse" for years, now clapping and cheering as he literally *exorcised his demons* with holy matrimony. Superstition can lead humans down some strange aisles, and this aisle was lined with paw prints.

As Selvakumar gently fed a piece of bun to his new "wife" in front of the cameras, you have to wonder: what was going through his mind? Relief at finally doing something to end his nightmare? Embarrassment mixed with hope? And what about poor Selvi – was she confused by all the fuss, or just happy to be the center of attention and snacks? Perhaps in the moment, it didn't matter. The deed was done, the curse (with any luck) lifted. Man and dog emerged from the temple as an official couple, at least in the eyes of the village and the cosmos. One can only imagine the conversation later that night: "So honey, how was your day? Bark once for good, twice for really weird."

Marriage Lesson: Treat your fellow creatures well – otherwise you might end up literally in the doghouse, reciting vows to a canine and shelling out for doggie diamonds. (Also, "till death do us part" feels a lot more ominous when you're trying to undo a curse!)

Ladies' Privilege – According to Irish tradition (dating back to St. Patrick), every Leap Year on February 29 women can propose marriage to men – a custom that once even had legal force in Europe

Gentlemen, consider yourselves warned: if it's Leap Year and February 29th rolls around, your girlfriend might just get down on one knee before you do. Don't say the Irish didn't warn you! The tradition commonly known as Bachelor's Day or Ladies' Privilege dates back over a millennium (or so the legends claim) and flips the script on the usual "waiting for him to propose" trope. In a nutshell: every four years, on that rare unicorn of a date – Feb 29 – women are "allowed" (oh, *thank you*, benevolent tradition) to propose marriage to men. In old Irish lore, this custom is attributed to none other than St. Patrick himself, with a little help from a persuasive Irish nun-turned-saint named Brigid. Story goes that Brigid complained to St. Pat that women were sick of sitting around while Mr. Right took his sweet time to pop the question. After what I imagine was some good-natured eye-rolling, St. Patrick offered a compromise: women could have one day – one day! – every few years to take matters (and kneeling cushions) into their own hands. Gee, what a guy.

Originally, the deal was one proposal day every seven years, but Brigid – being a sharp negotiator and knowing a raw deal when she saw one – bartered it down to every four years. (Apparently, even saints know how to haggle.) Thus, Leap Day proposals were born. And let's be clear, in the 5th century this was *revolutionary*. It was like giving women a one-day legal license to do something society normally frowned upon: assertively ask for a man's hand in marriage. Imagine all those medieval lords quaking in their chainmail every time Leap Year loomed near – "Good lord, Gerald, hide! It's the 29th and Lady Matilda's got *that look* in her eye!"

This quirky custom spread beyond Ireland, and at certain points in history it even had legal force. Legend has it that in 13th-century Scotland, a law (perhaps more myth than reality, but fun nonetheless) was passed under Queen Margaret's name, stating that if a man refused a woman's proposal on Leap Day, he had to pay a fine. And not just a slap on the wrist – the fines reportedly could be a silk dress or a dozen pairs of gloves for the lady in question. The idea was that the poor lass could hide the shame of her ringless finger behind all those gloves. (Because nothing soothes a broken heart like an excellent collection of evening gloves, right?) In some upper-crust European circles, this tradition persisted: a dude turning down a Leap Day proposal might owe a kiss, a fancy gown, or those twelve gloves to soften the blow. Basically, an old-school "thanks but no thanks" consolation prize. It's equal parts gallant and absurd – "I decline your hand, dear, but please enjoy these gloves as a token of my regret." Today that would be like someone rejecting your proposal but Venmo-ing you $500 for "emotional damages." Awfully civil, all things considered.

Throughout the centuries, Leap Day turned into a kind of pressure valve for the whole "marriage proposal" gender-role thing. By the 19th and 20th centuries, it was well entrenched in folklore and pop culture. Postcards from the early 1900s depict women chasing men with butterfly nets on Feb 29, tongue-in-cheek cartoons warning bachelors to lay low during Leap Year, and all manner of joking references to "Ladies' Privilege." It was a playful inversion of norms –

society's way of winking and saying, "Alright ladies, you get this one day to turn the tables. Have at it!"

Of course, in modern times, women don't need to wait for a magical date to propose. We've seen countless women ask the question on random Tuesdays in June, at baseball games, on hot air balloons, you name it – without the world ending or the guy fainting from shock. The whole Leap Year proposal thing now is more of a fun tradition, a nod to ye olden days when it *was* a big deal. (There was even a 2010 Amy Adams rom-com aptly titled "Leap Year" that threw this Irish custom into a cute road-trip love story – proving the idea still captures imaginations, or at least Hollywood screenwriters.) Some couples still embrace it for kicks: "We got engaged on Feb 29th, because I got tired of waiting and also hey, easy anniversary date to remember every four years!"

Cultural satire aside, you have to appreciate the Leap Day proposal tradition for its gentle subversiveness. It's like the Victorian-era version of Sadie Hawkins dances – a temporary role reversal that probably gave both men and women a little thrill. One can imagine eligible bachelors in 1800s England, sipping tea nervously as February wound down, aware that Miss Penelope might suddenly drop to one knee at the next garden party. And if he wasn't keen… well, better start saving up for those gloves or risk being the talk of the town. Scandalous!

Today, the "legal force" is gone (sorry ladies, you can't sue him for a silk dress if he says no), but the charm remains. Every Leap Year, newspapers trot out the history, lovebirds take advantage of the excuse to do something different, and a few brave women put on their proposing pants (or kilts, as the Irish tale would have it) and seize the day.

Marriage Lesson: Don't let outdated rules decide who can pop the question – if you love someone, go ahead and ask! (But if you *are* proposing on Feb 29, maybe have a nice pair of gloves ready... you know, just in case.)

Bachelor Tax – From Emperor Augustus's Rome to 20th-century governments, single men have been slapped with taxes for not marrying, as a not-so-subtle hint to get hitched

If you think *your* parents are pushy about you settling down, wait until you hear how governments throughout history have basically said, "So, no wife yet, huh? That'll be twenty bucks." Yes, the dreaded bachelor tax – a financial smack upside the head for unattached men – has popped up again and again over the last two millennia. It turns out that if Cupid's arrow can't get the job done, there's always Uncle Sam (or Emperor Augustus, or Mussolini) with an arrow of his own: a tax penalty for daring to remain single. Subtle as a sledgehammer.

The origin of this not-so-romantic revenue scheme goes back to Ancient Rome. Emperor Augustus Caesar – who, as ruler, apparently fancied himself Rome's top matchmaker – was deeply concerned about falling birth rates among the Roman elite and the moral decay of bachelorhood (or at least, that's the excuse he gave while counting coin). In 9 AD, he introduced the Lex Papia Poppaea, which can be summed up as: "Marry and make babies, or pay up, buddy." It levied taxes on unmarried men (between certain ages) *and* even on married couples with no kids. The message was clear: no heirs, no waifu, no lifeu... so we're coming for your denarii. One imagines Roman bachelors grumbling into their goblets of wine: "Great, now I have to find a wife or I can't afford my rent on the Palatine." Augustus's bachelor tax was part of a broader moral campaign – he was trying to legislate family values, boost population, and incidentally, fill the treasury (wars against barbarians aren't cheap, after all). Leave it to the Romans to make even marriage a civic duty enforced by the IRS (Imperial Revenue Service).

Fast forward to the 17th century, and the idea pops up in England. In 1695, under King William III, the government was strapped for cash (wars with France will do that) and thought, "Who has extra money lying around? Ah yes, those carefree bachelors!" Thus came the Marriage Duty Act, which among other fees, imposed a tax on single men over 25. It was essentially a "singleton surcharge" meant to refill the royal coffers and encourage those darned foot-dragging gentlemen to get hitched and start siring little taxpaying machines – er, children. This tax didn't last long (it was unpopular, shocker), but the logic behind it was a classic: incentivize marriage, disincentivize the wild life of the unattached male. Think of it as the crown's way of saying, "We're tired of waiting for your wedding invites; pay us in the meantime."

Bachelor taxes often had a not-so-thinly veiled moralistic vibe. Society has long held this (debatably misguided) notion that unmarried men are out there living the life of Riley – you know, drinking, gambling, generally having *too* good a time and not contributing to the wholesome fabric of family-based society. So why not profit from that or nudge them toward the altar with a little financial prod? Case in point: South Africa in 1919 slapped a tax on bachelors to encourage white men to marry and multiply – a policy entangled with racist population politics of that era. Nothing says romance like "Do it for the demographic supremacy, boys!"

And then we have the hall-of-famer of bachelor-bashers: Benito Mussolini. In 1927, Il Duce looked around fascist Italy, saw too many single men loafing about (in his view), and basically said "*Basta!* This is not the Roman Empire I idolize." Mussolini's regime imposed a steep bachelor tax on men (age 25 and up, with exemptions for the clergy and some other cases) to both fund the government and, in theory, spur population growth for a mightier Italy. It was a double-whammy of authoritarian matchmaking and fundraising. Mussolini even gave florid speeches equating bachelorhood with selfishness and decay. He wanted more Italian babies and less "lazy" bachelors sipping espressos solo. So if you were an unmarried Italian man in the late 1920s, you suddenly found yourself paying extra lire each year for the privilege of flying solo – a "single and not loving it" tax. Many grudgingly married to avoid the tax (romantic!), while others paid up and likely groused that it was still cheaper than a wedding and a mother-in-law.

The United States also toyed with the idea, proving that even the land of the free wasn't above nagging its single men via tax code. In the 1860s and again around World War I, a few U.S. states proposed or enacted small bachelor taxes. Missouri supposedly had a $1 bachelor tax in 1821 (one dollar – high enough for a couple of beers, so not exactly life-ruining). Michigan debated it multiple times in the 19th century, often with tongue-in-cheek legislators arguing, "If we're gonna tax the men, tax the single ladies too!" (Ah, equal opportunity pestering.) In Montana, believe it or not, a bachelor tax *actually passed* in 1921 – $3 a year on every unmarried man over 21. That might buy you, like, 10 gallons of gas back then, so it stung a bit. California flirted with a hefty $25 bachelor tax in the 1930s to encourage marriages during the Depression (imagine, "Marry a wife, save on taxes" billboards on Route 66), but it never became law. Generally, in the U.S., bachelor taxes were either short-lived or failed because – surprise – people accused them of being grossly unfair, discriminatory, and frankly a government overreach into personal lives. The bachelors of yore weren't exactly mounting armed rebellions over $3, but they did pen some fiery newspaper editorials. One journalist quipped that any man scared into marriage by a tax "would lack the nerve and stamina to make a good husband anyway." In other words, if a $3 fee is the only thing pushing you to say "I do," maybe you're not cut out for the long haul of matrimony, pal.

In hindsight, the bachelor tax is almost comical: the state acting like a *yenta* with a calculator. "What, no wife yet? Tsk tsk, that'll cost you. Maybe you'll think twice next time you pass a jewelry store." It's a mix of moral policing and revenue grabbing that seems straight out of a dystopian satire. And yet, the fact it kept resurfacing suggests it struck a chord (or struck gold) for those in power. Today, we have more subtle versions – tax *breaks* for married folks, for instance, which effectively penalize singles in some systems. (The IRS won't send you a note saying "Get married already," but your tax refund might.)

All in all, the bachelor tax stands as one of those stranger-than-fiction policies that actually existed. It's a testament to how obsessively society has tried to herd people toward marriage, like prodding reluctant sheep. The next time your grandma asks when you're finally going to settle down, be glad she's not then handing you a bill for remaining single. And if Uncle Sam ever resurrects the bachelor tax, expect a lot of quick courthouse weddings – or a sharp rise in guys claiming to be monks.

Marriage Lesson: True love can't be forced – and if governments try to charge you for staying single, it might be time to swipe right *real* fast... or just move to a place with lower taxes on your independence.

The Big "I Do" – In 1992, 20,825 couples said "I do" in unison at a Seoul stadium (with 9,800 more couples via satellite) in history's largest mass wedding – talk about married at first sight

How do you take your wedding? Intimate ceremony on a beach? Rustic barn with close family? How about in a giant Olympic stadium with *20,000+ other couples* simultaneously saying "I do" in a chorus that could shake the rafters? Welcome to the world's largest mass wedding ever recorded – the mother of all matrimony, the "Big Bang" of weddings, the moment when 20,825 couples got hitched in one fell swoop, with nearly 10,000 more pairs joining virtually from other countries. If ever there was a Guinness World Record for "Most Champagne Toasts at Once" or "Largest collective cold feet," this was it.

The date was August 25, 1992. The place: Seoul, South Korea at the Olympic Stadium. But this wasn't a sporting event – unless you consider matrimony an extreme sport (and honestly, some might). It was organized by the late Reverend Sun Myung Moon's Unification Church, famous (or infamous) for these colossal "blessing ceremonies." Imagine the scene: over 40,000 individuals – brides in flowing white gowns and grooms in dark suits – filling the stands and the field, a sea of tulle, veils, and nervously cheery faces. Overhead, perhaps the bluest sky, and on the stage, Rev. Moon and his wife, dressed like royalty, literally wearing crowns, presiding over the whole shebang. It's like someone merged the Super Bowl halftime show with a royal wedding and then said, "You know what, let's *10x* it." No celebrity wedding, no matter how many Instagram followers, holds a candle to this sheer scale of "I do."

At the crucial moment, Reverend Moon (the self-declared matchmaker-in-chief, and according to his followers, the *Messiah* of marital harmony) spoke into the microphone and asked the throngs of couples to affirm their vows. You can imagine the pause, the collective inhale. Then, in unison, 20,000+ grooms and brides shouted "YES!" or "I do!" in their multitude of languages, and it echoed like a wave through the stadium. Observers said it sounded like a massive cheer, the kind you'd hear when an underdog scores a winning goal. One can only hope the audio guy had the levels set *real* low on those mics. Talk about surround sound – Dolby Atmos has nothing on thousands of lovebirds pledging eternal devotion all at once.

What makes this even more fantastically bizarre is that many of these couples had met each other only days (or hours) before the ceremony. Most were paired up by Rev. Moon himself, who was known to play celestial matchmaker by reviewing photos and biodata of followers from around the world. Imagine flying into Seoul and meeting your future spouse at the airport for the first time: "Hi, nice to meet you. Ready to get married in front of, oh, the whole world on live satellite TV tomorrow? Cool." It's married at first sight on steroids. Reality TV has since tried concepts like this (looking at you, *Married* at *First Sight* and *Love Is Blind*), but even those shows have the courtesy to marry off people a dozen at a time, not *tens of thousands*. Rev. Moon was essentially running the ultimate blind date megamarathon, trusting that love (and shared faith) would find a way to bloom amidst the synchronized confetti.

The logistics of the event were mind-boggling. Think of the coordinators trying to line up 20,000 brides and grooms: "Couple #18,562, you're in row 37, seats 8 A and B. Don't be late!" Did they print that many programs? Were there enough porta-potties? What about *wedding cake* – was there a single colossal cake or did everyone get a cupcake? The mind reels. Photos show happy couples, some beaming ear to ear, some looking a tad shell-shocked (understandable, given the circumstances). When the officiation was done, there was likely a synchronized kiss – hopefully you got the *right* spouse in the melee! – and cheers from an audience full of parents, friends, and curious onlookers in the stands. The stadium steps became an endless backdrop for wedding photos. I bet the local florists and tux rental shops had their best sales day in history. And imagine being a caterer asked to handle the post-wedding reception: "So how many guests?" "Oh, about 100,000…" *Gulp.*

This 1992 mega-wedding was so large it made the Guinness Book of World Records. It wasn't Rev. Moon's first mass wedding rodeo, and it wouldn't be the last (later events in the '90s would involve even more couples, if you can believe it). But this one stands out for its iconic imagery and the era – pre-Internet, so people were *faxing* in their congratulations. Yet, it was broadcast by satellite to couples abroad who participated remotely, making it a kind of early experiment in "virtual wedding attendance." Zoom weddings have nothing on this –

the Moonies pioneered the concept by hooking up thousands of lovebirds via satellite feed decades before anyone dreamed of live-streaming nuptials from Vegas.

Cultural reaction to this event was a mix of awe, skepticism, and joking envy. Awe at the sheer commitment (pun intended) to organize something of this magnitude. Skepticism from those who dubbed the Unification Church a cult and wondered if these youngsters really knew what they were signing up for (both in terms of spouse and religion). And envy from wedding planners who probably thought, "If only I could get a commission on that event…". Comedians had a field day too – Jay Leno quipped on *The Tonight Show* that year about the world's largest wedding and likely the world's largest wedding bill. Can you fathom the group discount they must have gotten on catering and venues? Possibly the only wedding in history where *stadium seating* was literal.

For the couples, though, it was deadly earnest. This was a sacred moment, one they believed would tie them not just to each other but into a greater global family under Rev. Moon's spiritual vision. Many of those marriages lasted, some didn't – pretty much like any cross-section of 20,000 marriages, I suppose. But for one sweltering summer day in Seoul, they were part of something indelibly extraordinary. If nothing else, every anniversary is a chance to say, "Honey, remember when we got married with 20,824 other couples? Beat that, Kardashians."

Marriage Lesson: Love can be a numbers game, but whether you're one in a million or a million in one stadium, a marriage still comes down to two people. It's not the size of the ceremony that matters – it's finding your own *special someone* in the crowd and holding on tight, even if 20,000 other pairs of lips are locking at the exact same moment as yours. Cheers to that – and pass the champagne (all 20,825 bottles of it)!

Epilogue

After parading you through a global gauntlet of bizarre betrothals and dramatic divorces, we've finally reached our happily-ever-after (or not) at the end of this book. What a journey it's been! We've laughed, we've winced, and perhaps even wiped away a tear (or was that just a drop of leftover toilet-bowl wedding punch?). When it comes to tying and untying the knot across civilizations, humanity has truly done it all – for better, for worse, and yes, mostly bizarre.

Across continents, the pageantry of saying "I do" proved that no tradition is too absurd. In Congo, couples must suppress every smile on their wedding day, while in South Korea the groom's pals literally flog his feet with a raw fish to prepare him for married life.

We encountered brides literally tied to a tree and pelted with garbage by their own loved ones to prove they can handle anything marriage throws their way. Some French newlyweds had to chug a stew of wedding leftovers straight from a toilet bowl (suddenly the bouquet toss seems tame). And lest we snicker too loudly, let's not forget the Las Vegas chapels with Elvis impersonators officiating drive-thru weddings – absurdity knows no borders.

Even ending a marriage comes with its own theatrics. In Mauritania, a divorced woman is serenaded back into single life with ululating songs of joy – sometimes a faux suitor performs to make her ex jealous. In 19th-century England, one husband literally auctioned off his wife at the village market for a shilling (who needs lawyers when you've got an auctioneer?).

So what's the final takeaway from this matrimonial circus? People everywhere can't resist wrapping their biggest commitments in spectacle – the crazier, the better. The absurdity has a purpose: beneath the costumes and flying dishes, these customs help us cope with the daunting promise of "forever" and the gut-punch of "not anymore." We've seen people turn fear into fun and pain into poetry, proving that hope and humor can wear even the weirdest disguises. If nothing else, love – in all its bizarre glory – remains the one circus everyone is eager to join.

Writing this book made us equal, parts anthropologist and court jester, and I hope you enjoyed the ride. Thank you for laughing and learning with us along the way. We will never look at a wedding (or a divorce party) the same way again – and we will be smiling (unless we are at a Congolese wedding). Here's to love, laughter, and the human talent for finding meaning in madness.

Yours truly,

Nicci & Ben